THE
15-
MINUTE
VEGETARIAN
GOURMET

Also by Paulette Mitchell

The New American Vegetarian Menu Cookbook

THE 15-MINUTE VEGETARIAN GOURMET

PAULETTE MITCHELL

*Illustrations by Barbara Fiore
and Mary Garrity*

Collier Books   Macmillan Publishing Company   New York

Maxwell Macmillan Canada   Toronto

Maxwell Macmillan International
New York   Oxford   Singapore   Sydney

◆

Collier Books
Macmillan Publishing Company
866 Third Avenue
New York, NY 10022

Maxwell Macmillan Canada, Inc.
1200 Eglinton Avenue East
Suite 200
Don Mills, Ontario M3C 3N1

Macmillan Publishing Company is part of the Maxwell Communication Group of Companies.

Library of Congress Cataloging-in-Publication Data

Mitchell, Paulette.
    The 15-minute vegetarian gourmet / Paulette Mitchell. — 1st Collier Books ed.
      p.   cm.
    Includes index.
    ISBN 0-02-009815-4
    1. Vegetarian cookery.   I. Title.
TX837.M64 1992
641.5'636—dc20   91-34846   CIP

Macmillan books are available at special discounts for bulk purchases for sales promotions, premiums, fund-raising, or educational use. For details, contact:

Special Sales Director
Macmillan Publishing Company
866 Third Avenue
New York, NY 10022

First Collier Books Edition 1992

10 9 8 7 6 5 4 3 2

Printed in the United States of America

To my son, Brett,
who, at age three, tested my recipes as well as my patience.

CONTENTS

PREFACE *ix*

1 THE VEGETARIAN COOK *1*

2 BASICS *11*

3 APPETIZERS *29*

4 SOUPS *39*

5 SALADS *55*

6 ENTREES *81*

7 DESSERTS *117*

8 THE VEGETARIAN ENTERTAINER *137*

9 HOW TO PLAN A VEGETARIAN MEAL *139*

INDEX *143*

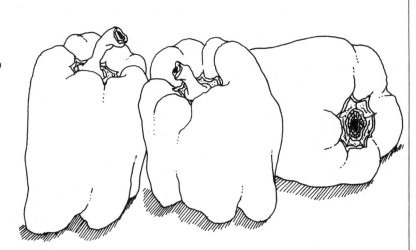

PREFACE

Several years ago I began teaching people how to cook vegetarian dishes. The question most often asked of me then was, How can you make a vegetarian menu exciting? I answered that question in my first book, *The New American Vegetarian Menu Cookbook*. A few years later, with people busier than ever, the question most often asked of me was, Doesn't it take a long time to cook vegetarian meals? The answer, of course, was yes, it often *does* take more time—to shop for the freshest ingredients; to plan nutritious, interesting meals; and to chop, dice, and blend those glorious, fresh ingredients into a mouth-watering dish.

As I became busier, it became a challenge to me to develop exciting new meatless dishes that could be prepared with a minimum of fuss, yet still be decidedly "gourmet" and, above all else, healthful. These recipes are not meant to replace your collection of favorites and classics but to enhance your repertoire and save you time.

As I developed the recipes in this book, I also devised kitchen strategies that go hand in hand with the 15-minute approach to vegetarian cooking. All of the recipes are easy to follow and make use of readily available ingredients. There are "ethnic" touches throughout, and many of the recipes are speedy adaptations of more complicated classic dishes.

Vegetarian cuisine is a natural for the 15-minute approach: vegetables are at their peak of flavor and nutrition when cooked only until crisp-tender and herbs are their most pungent when not overcooked.

And nothing has been sacrificed along the way. The cook who utilizes the "quick" approach to vegetarian cooking will still be using mostly fresh, natural ingredients to create exciting meals. But he or she will be creating them in one-quarter the time.

I have found this new streamlined approach to vegetarian cooking has really worked for me: I now have more time to teach, exercise, and be with my family and friends. I hope this book frees you from long hours in the kitchen and adds nutrition and style to everything you prepare.

—PAULETTE MITCHELL

1

THE VEGETARIAN COOK

You do not need to be a strict vegetarian to enjoy the pleasures of meatless cuisine. The vegetarian dishes in this book have enough variety, taste, texture, and beauty to appeal to the staunchest defender of meat-and-potatoes.

Times have changed, and more and more people are willing to try everything from tofu to couscous—provided, of course, that it is presented well and tastes delicious.

My decision to become a vegetarian was not a moral one. My husband and I tried vegetarianism twelve years ago as an experiment: we wanted to enhance our health. As we eliminated meat from our diet, we also cut back on salt, sugar, and excess fat and added more fiber. We combined our new interest in healthful eating with a plan for overall fitness. Daily exercise became a part of our lives, and after a few years I became an aerobics instructor so that I could share my enthusiasm with others.

During this turnaround in our lives I took many cooking classes, but found many of them too traditional to conform to our new way of eating. Sauces were too rich, ingredients often unhealthful and difficult to find. French and Chinese cooking classes appealed to me most and led me to the "gourmet" approach. I found that many ethnic dishes contained no meat—or when meat was used it was a flavoring rather than a source of protein. I was also attracted to the various combinations of herbs and spices that eliminated the need to add salt. I found myself experimenting in the kitchen, inventing new dishes, and trying out different flavors, always using the freshest ingredients I could find. It was a real challenge, but it became enormously rewarding to surprise and delight my family and friends with gourmet meals that contained no meat, low-fat ingredients, no salt, and little or no sugar.

Over the ten years I have instructed classes in healthy eating, I have become increasingly aware that *total vegetarianism is not for everyone*. However, I have seen a definite trend toward healthier eating. Many people are voluntarily reducing their meat intake in favor of a more whole-food, plant-based diet and are making various healthful changes in their diets. Although they initially worry about missing what they are "giving up" as meat becomes secondary in their meal planning, they are usually amazed by what they gain! A prudent meatless diet is merely a substitution of one set of food patterns for another.

There is really nothing complicated or mysterious about vegetarian cuisine. I have passed on a few basic principles to my students that I think may be generally helpful. If you follow these three principles, adapting them as you see fit, you'll be well on your way to a healthier way of eating.

1. BALANCE

Ideally, each meal of the day should contain some of all the essential nutrients—protein, carbohydrates, and fats.

◆ The average American diet is often very high in *protein*; however, nutritionists are now pointing out the benefits of changing food intake to 60 percent carbohydrate, 30 percent fat, and 10 percent protein. The challenge for the nutritionally aware vegetarian cook is to find other sources of protein besides red meat. Surprising to many people is the fact that it is not difficult to consume equivalent high quality protein on a meatless diet. This can be as simple as including tofu or egg, which are complete proteins on their own. Also certain other meatless foods can combine to form complete protein. The following food combinations should be kept in mind when planning your menus. I have provided examples from the recipes in this book.

Grains and Milk Products (you need less dairy than grain)
- Macaroni and Cheese with Vegetables (p. 92)
- Triple Cheese–Poppyseed Noodles (p. 91)
- Couscous with Egg Sauce and Garden Vegetables (p. 114)

Grains and Legumes (in relatively equal amounts)
- Pasta and Bean Soup (p. 46)
- Chick Pea–Zucchini Curry on pasta or rice (p. 87)

Seeds and Legumes
- Hummus (p. 32)
- Moroccan Chick Pea Soup (p. 47)
- Teriyaki Salad (p. 71)

Eggs, milk, and tofu are complete proteins on their own, but the quality of protein is further enhanced in these recipes:
- Oriental Rice and Vegetable Skillet (p. 111)
- Pasta with Ricotta-Walnut Sauce (p. 86)
- Sweet and Sour Tofu on rice (p. 94)

- Noodle Omelet with Ricotta Filling (pp. 102–3)

- *Carbohydrates* are the only nutrient providing energy alone. Simple carbohydrates, such as sucrose, corn syrup, molasses, lactose, and fruits, offer quick energy but some are found in foods containing few other nutrients. The exception is fruits, which can be rich sources of vitamins, minerals, and fiber. Complex carbohydrates, such as cereals, pastas, rice, and legumes, are low in calories, contain some protein, and are rich sources of vitamins, minerals, and fiber without adding excess fat.

- *Fats* are a necessary part of cell structure and carry fat-soluble vitamins. They also add flavor to foods. However, they should be used in moderation. Fats are divided into three groups: saturated, unsaturated, or monosaturated. Saturated fats are found in both plant and animal foods: meat lard, butter, coconut oil, and palm oil. They are usually solid at room temperature and have been shown to raise the levels of serum cholesterol and to increase the risk of heart disease and certain cancers. Unsaturated fats, such as safflower oil, corn oil, soy oil, and sesame oil, are usually liquid at room temperature. They are the best to use and actually reduce blood cholesterol. Monosaturated fats, such as olive oil and peanut oil, have no effect on cholesterol levels.

- *Water* is yet another nutrient, actually the most important to life. An added benefit of eating plenty of fresh fruits and vegetables is that they have a very high water content.

With the current emphasis on increasing the public awareness of osteoporosis (degenerative bone disease), the importance of consuming dairy products is being stressed. While dairy products do provide calcium, which is important in the prevention of this disease, they are also an important source of complete protein, especially for the vegetarian cook. The quality of protein is the same in high-fat products, such as cream or whole milk, as it is in skim milk. But I recommend using low-fat dairy products, and my recipes have been developed with this in mind.

Balance also refers to the balance of raw and cooked foods. Fresh raw food often contains more of its original nutrients than cooked food because some vitamins are destroyed by heat and others are dispersed into the cooking liquid. It is a good idea to try to make at least one raw food or salad a part of your daily menu.

2. VARIETY

You have probably heard since grade school that a balanced diet requires you to select foods from each of the four basic food groups: dairy, grains, vegetables and fruits, and protein. True enough. But did you know that by eating from all of the food groups you may still not ingest all of the needed nutrients? To consume all of your needed vitamins and nutrients, you need to eat a variety of foods from each of the food groups.

I like to think that the vegetarian gourmet approach encourages variety. Since you are no longer using meat as the focus of your meals, you naturally cook with a wide variety of fruits, vegetables, grains, and legumes—and with the increased availability of exotic foods and fresh produce, you have a veritable treasure chest at hand. Most important, once you become an educated eater, you are more aware of the nutrients in the foods you eat.

Fiber:

In processing, one of the elements often removed from foods is fiber. Whole wheat products and brown rice are high in fiber, as are fruits and vegetables. The benefits of fiber are unaffected by cooking: raw or cooked, it has the same value. Some researchers think fiber plays an important role in the prevention of heart disease and cancer.

3. MODERATION

This is the hardest principle for Americans to learn. Many of us are plagued by our own excesses: too much salt, too much sugar, too much caffeine, too much fat, too many processed foods with additives. Whatever your "excess," the key is to discover it and eliminate it.

Salt:

The daily sodium requirement is about $\frac{1}{10}$ teaspoon; the average intake is 1 to 4 teaspoons daily! Excessive salt intake has been shown to lead to hypertension, which in turn is related to numerous potential health problems. The recipes in this book add no salt, so if you are a heavy salter you may be tempted to reach for the saltshaker. Once you become aware of the delights of herbs and fresh flavors, your need for salt will diminish and you will enjoy exploring other tastes. Our desire for salty food is a learned behavior that can be unlearned. Give it time.

Sugar:
The average American consumes 120 pounds of processed sugar a year. That is 1 pound every three days, most of which comes from processed foods. Because processed sugar is usually found in low-nutrition, high-fat foods, it does not contribute anything to our diet except excess calories and, hence, excess body fat. Problems develop when highly sugared foods replace nutritious foods in the diet. Some experts even believe that sugar may affect blood cholesterol levels and be a factor in coronary heart disease.

Additives:
Several thousand chemical substances are currently added to our foods during manufacture to preserve, flavor, and color them. There is conflicting evidence as to their effects, but many are thought to be potentially harmful. Begin to read labels and be aware of what is in the foods you buy. Keep in mind that by using unprocessed, natural ingredients you have more control over the content of your foods.

Fats:
If you are planning meatless meals, dairy products will become an important source of protein. With evidence on the relationship between cholesterol and coronary heart disease, low-fat products are usually recommended. I have used no cream or whole milk and have provided suggestions for the elimination of egg yolks whenever possible.

With all of these concerns, at times one begins to wonder, "What can I eat with a clear conscience?" Recipes in this book do limit salts and fats; unsaturated fats are recommended and are used in moderation. Sugar has been kept to a minimum. Natural, unprocessed foods are used wherever possible because the closer food is to the state in which it is grown, the more nutritious it will be. Remember, it is not necessary to eliminate if you cut down. The key word is moderation.

THE FIFTEEN-MINUTE COOK: HOW IT WORKS

I am assuming that if you are using this book, you are drawn to the idea of "cooking from scratch," yet do not have the time or even the desire to spend long hours in the kitchen. This is good, because the 15-minute recipes—and that includes chopping time!—rely more on an imaginative use of fresh ingredients than on elaborate technique. The substantial main courses require less emphasis on side dishes and many courses. You will not spend a great deal of time cooking—but no one will ever know it. Using the freshest ingredients in an organized manner, you will achieve amazing results with minimum effort.

THE WEEKLY PLAN

The key to successful 15-minute vegetarian gourmet cooking is advance planning. Keep a running list of staples tacked inside a kitchen cabinet and add to it as you run out. Plan the week's menus and make a list of the fresh ingredients you need to purchase. With your two lists in hand, make your weekly trip to the supermarket. Advance planning enables you to use up fresh ingredients before they spoil and guarantees that you will have what you need when you need it.

THE ORGANIZED KITCHEN

The size of your kitchen does not matter; the way you make it work for you does. The more efficient your kitchen, the more capable and relaxed you are likely to feel. Store utensils close to where they are to be used. Arrange spices in alphabetical order near the stove. Store knives nearest the cutting board. Store frequently used items in visible places so you can find—and grab—them quickly. Occasionally, this may mean having doubles of certain items such as mixing bowls and measuring spoons.

THE BASICS ON HAND

Although vegetarian cuisine depends upon a lot of chopping, dicing, and general food preparation, you *can* make some of the basics—vegetable stock and mustard, for example—ahead of time, *when you have the time.* It is a good idea to keep a supply of the basics on hand so you are ready at a moment's notice to prepare a dish.

THE PLANNED PRESENTATION

Allow more than a few minutes to think about presentation. As you plan your meal, select one or two of the garnishes I have suggested. You can be a quick, efficient cook, but your meals should not look slap-dash. Serve pasta salads on lovely platters. Adorn them with fresh herbs, fruits, or whatever pleases your eye. A garnish of fresh mint or fresh basil takes only a few seconds—and some imagination. When you know a few simple tricks of the trade, your meals will look as though they were prepared by a trained gourmet rather than a hurried cook.

THE EQUIPMENT AT ITS BEST

You do not need an elaborate kitchen in order to be a 15-minute gourmet cook. However, a careful selection of practical equipment *will* speed up the process. Buy the best equipment you can afford. Commercial quality pots and pans are initially quite expensive but they will last a lifetime. The same is true of knives. Quality knives will cost more now, but you will not have to replace them in two or three years. I also find—and my students agree—that quality equipment has a special feel and adds to the pleasure of cooking.

TEN TIPS FOR FLAWLESS 15-MINUTE COOKING

Throughout this book there are hints, tips, and practical suggestions to help you become a better 15-minute cook. Here are ten to get you started:

- Do some of the week's food preparations in advance. Chop onions, grate cheese, chop nuts, and store in tightly covered containers in the refrigerator.
- When possible, begin with ingredients at room temperature; for items that are to be served chilled, keep ingredients in the refrigerator until ready to be used.
- Bring water to a boil faster by covering the pot with a lid.
- Read the recipe carefully before you begin! Gather all the ingredients together before you start to cook.
- Add ingredients to the cooking pan as they are prepared, as suggested in many recipes in this book.
- Cover the pan to make foods cook more quickly.
- Chop vegetables in similar sizes so they will cook at the same rate.
- When doubling a recipe, use two pans, side by side, so that the entire recipe will be done at the same time.
- Particularly when entertaining, chop or shred some ingredients ahead of time.

- Always preheat the oil before sautéing. The food will cook faster and absorb less oil.

THE TEN TECHNIQUES FOR THE 15-MINUTE VEGETARIAN COOK

FOOD PROCESSING

A food processor is the one appliance that is necessary for the 15-minute cook. It makes short work of chopping nuts, grating cheese, and pureeing soups and sauces. Look at every recipe with the food processor in mind. Cleanup is easier if you do not have to wash the bowl after each use: just remember to process strong foods, like onions, last. And, when possible, chop dry foods first, then wet foods.

If you do not have a food processor, many of the procedures, such as blending or pureeing, can be done in your blender. The process may require doing the task in several smaller batches which will require more time. Also, the consistency will not be as pleasing as when using a food processor, resulting in a lesser quality end product. Some procedures, such as grating or shredding, simply cannot be done in a blender and will need to be done by hand.

When you are selecting a food processor, as with all kitchen equipment, buy the best you can afford. High-quality food processors have stability, smooth operation, powerful motors, and long-lasting accessories making them well worth the added cost in the long run.

CHOPPING BY HAND

When time permits and when I prefer precisely sliced or chopped food, I often use my knives rather than my food processor. Chopping is the most important technique in vegetarian cooking and it begins with a good, sharp knife. Fewer accidents occur with sharp knives; and the sharper the knife, the faster you will work. It is a good idea to sharpen your knife after each use.

The proper use of a French chef's knife will hasten any procedure. Begin with a good cutting board and do all the cutting with the broad end of the blade, near the handle, using short, up and down motions and moving the knife in a circle so that it traverses all of the food to be minced, sliced, or chopped. Learn to cut large quantities at once, never just one stalk of celery or carrot unless you need only one. Dice by chopping in checkerboard fashion so that each swipe of the knife cuts 8 to 10 cubes.

SAUTÉING

This is a speedy method for cooking food in a low-sided pan atop the stove, using as little fat as possible. Sautéing is a terrific technique for the 15-minute cook, particularly in the preparation of soups and skillet dishes. Sautéing the vegetables before adding them to the pot eliminates the need for lengthy simmering and also adds flavor. When you sauté, preheat the oil before you add the food. Also, make sure the food is dry before it is added to the hot oil.

STIR-FRYING

This technique is similar to sautéing with the added step of stirring the food constantly and briskly as it cooks.

BROILING

This method traditionally involves cooking the food in an oven broiler, directly under the heat source.

COLD-TOSSING

Used mostly in salad preparation, this technique involves the tossing together of ingredients away from a heat source.

SCRAMBLING

Most often used for egg mixtures, scrambling means cooking gently in fat, lifting portions of food as they cook to allow uncooked portions to flow beneath.

STEAMING

Steaming is the process of cooking food in a porous receptacle over a small amount of water. Stainless-steel steamers or Oriental bamboo steamers usually work best, allowing the steam generated by the water to circulate around and through the food. Be sure to use a tight-fitting lid to prevent steam (and nutrients) from escaping.

MICROWAVING

I use my microwave most often for reheating leftovers, though several procedures in this book can be accomplished in a microwave. Vegetables, for example, can be microwaved instead of steamed with equal efficiency and good results. Just be careful not to overcook them.

PRESSURE COOKING

Though I do not use a pressure cooker, some of the recipes can be adapted successfully for its use. It is a time-saving option in the preparation of such basics as vegetable stock and legumes.

STOCKING THE 15-MINUTE GOURMET PANTRY

Supermarket shopping once a week should be enough for staples, but you may have to go one additional time to stock up on fresh ingredients. You can do most of your shopping in the outer perimeter of the supermarket, where fresh fruits, fresh vegetables, and dairy products are shelved. For useful staples such as canned tomatoes, canned beans, frozen juice concentrates, nuts, and rice, you will need to venture inward; however, when time permits you might want to purchase these items in bulk at a good neighborhood food co-op or health food store.

FRESH, FROZEN, OR CANNED?

Most of the recipes in this book have been developed using fresh, natural ingredients, which are readily available. But certain frozen and canned foods are helpful and acceptable for the 15-minute cook: frozen peas, because of the time it takes to shell fresh ones; canned beans in recipes calling for legumes (drain and rinse them first to remove excess salt); canned tomato paste, tomato sauce, and whole tomatoes (salt-free varieties, if possible). Also keep in mind that many of the ingredients in vegetarian recipes can be varied to suit your preferences or to use available produce.

When using commercially prepared products, *always read the labels carefully.* Many manufacturers have responded to consumer demand for low-sodium and sodium-free canned products, and the labels will provide this information. Though labeling standards are constantly being refined, at present the U.S. government has no definitions for the terms "low-fat," "natural," or "organic." *Read the fine print!*

Vegetable stock, which is used in many recipes in this book, can be made from scratch ahead of time and frozen for later use (see p. 12). However, I nearly always use vegetable stock powder.

Recipes in this book use dried herbs unless fresh are specified. I like to use fresh herbs, however, when they are available. Although they are expensive, many varieties of fresh herbs can be purchased year-round at quality supermarkets or specialty stores. If you cannot find them, you can easily grow some, either in your garden or indoors on your windowsill. When substituting fresh herbs for dried, use three times the amount called for in the recipe.

As for leftovers, I prefer creative uses for them over freezing. The quality and texture of foods nearly always deteriorate after being frozen and thawed, which diminishes the benefits of beginning with fresh ingredients. Furthermore, with a wealth of 15-minute recipes, there are few needs for freezing.

A WORD ABOUT OILS

I am very particular about oils. I recommend "cold-pressed oils" because heat processing destroys many of an oil's natural nutrients. Generally, cold-pressed oils are preservative-free and therefore must be stored in the refrigerator. I use a cold-pressed safflower oil for most recipes. Its very mild flavor is compatible with most ingredients. It is the best source of polyunsaturated fats among the oils, and it naturally contains lecithin, which helps to emulsify fats. It also has a high smoking point which makes it ideal for sautéing and frying.

Though I usually use cold-pressed oils, sesame oil is an exception. Cold-pressed sesame oil simply does not have the flavor of regular sesame oil. Dark sesame oils (or toasted sesame oils) have a stronger aroma and a more intense flavor. Add 1 tablespoon or less near the end of cooking to give a nutty aroma to soups, sauces, or sautéed food. Sesame oil can be purchased in the ethnic section of supermarkets or in Oriental groceries. It should be stored in the refrigerator, where it will keep for up to 6 months.

The finest olive oil is very pale yellow. It comes from the first pressings of the olives and is more expensive than oil from the second and third pressings; they are progressively darker in color and heavier in flavor. I also select regular olive oil rather than cold-pressed.

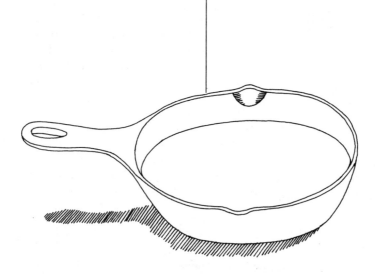

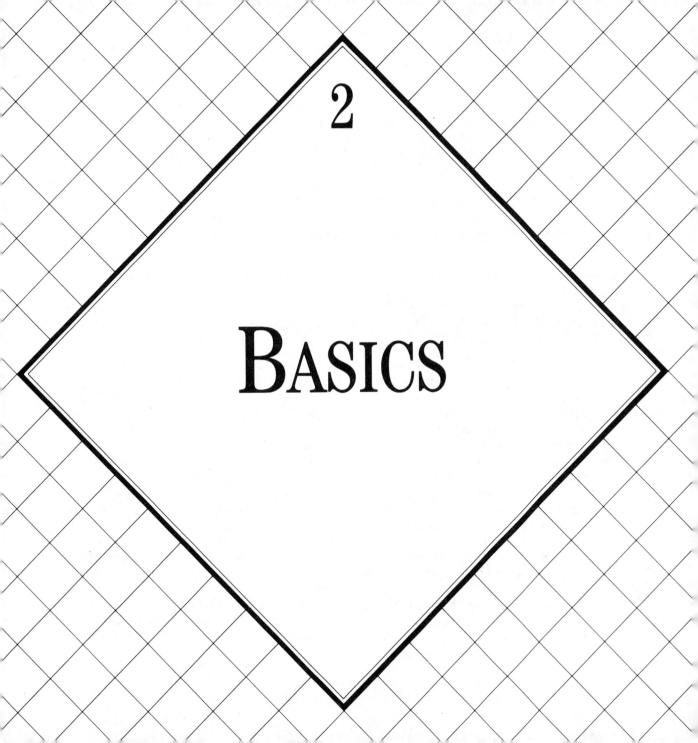

2

BASICS

Some of the foods I call "the basics" are commercially available, so you may wonder why you need to make them "from scratch." Once you've tasted homemade mayonnaise and mustard, you will know why.

Do-ahead staples such as rice and legumes will save you time when you want to be a 15-minute cook. Other basics such as vegetable stock can also be prepared ahead of time and refrigerated (or frozen) for later use.

Sauces are "basic" because they are used in a variety of recipes, both those in this book and others you may develop on your own. And basic techniques such as omelet-making and the preparation of pasta and grains are a must for using this book.

VEGETABLE STOCK

In many recipes, the key to rich flavor is good stock. Many of the commercially prepared stocks and cubes contain salt and other additives. If, however, you really do not have time to make your own, health food stores sell a variety of healthful stock cubes and granules. I use them often.

If you have the time (15 minutes to prepare plus 1 hour to simmer), try the following recipe. It can be varied to use whatever vegetables you have on hand. Remember, the key to good stock is to achieve a balance of flavors without any single one predominating. Asparagus, broccoli, cabbage, and cauliflower create very strong flavors and should be used sparingly, if at all. The same holds true for starchy vegetables such as corn, peas, or potatoes: they can cloud the broth. Parsnips and carrots will create a sweeter stock.

Vegetables to be used in stock should not be peeled, but they should be trimmed of any bruises. Cut vegetables into large chunks; small pieces may disintegrate and make the broth cloudy.

To vary the flavor of the stock, herbs may be added, although I recommend seasoning the stock sparingly: herbs are usually added to recipes in which the stock is later used. For a less intense flavor, add vegetables to the water in the pot *without sautéing*. For a more intense flavor, return the strained stock to the pot and simmer, uncovered, over low heat for an additional 30 minutes to 1 hour.

Stock is easily made ahead because it freezes well. For smaller quantities, try freezing the stock in ice cube trays, then remove the cubes and use them as needed.

ADVANCE PREPARATION

Stock may be used immediately, refrigerated for 3 to 4 days, or frozen up to 1 month.

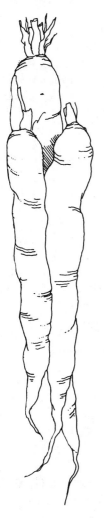

VEGETABLE STOCK

2 tablespoons safflower oil
1 large onion, sliced
1 carrot, sliced (greens may be included)
1 stalk celery, sliced (greens may be included)
1 tomato, cubed
1 potato, cubed
1 turnip, sliced (peel if waxed)
2 cloves garlic, halved
2 quarts plus 1 cup water
1 bay leaf
1 large sprig parsley
1/2 teaspoon black pepper

In a stock pot, heat oil. Add onion, carrot, celery, tomato, potato, turnip, and garlic. Cook until vegetables are tender, about 10 minutes.

Add remaining ingredients. Cover, bring to a boil, reduce heat, and simmer for 1 hour.

Strain stock and discard the vegetables, bay leaf, and parsley.

makes 2 quarts

GRAINS

RICE

Like pasta, rice is low in calories—and it is enormously versatile. Furthermore, when combined with legumes, seeds, or dairy products it forms a complete protein. I recommend long-grain brown rice because it contains three times the dietary fiber of white rice and more vitamins, minerals, and protein. It also separates more easily after cooking and makes a fluffier rice.

White rice has a slightly shorter cooking time than brown rice. Some people prefer the flavor and texture of white rice. But do not substitute *instant* white rice. It is not only inferior in flavor and texture, but is also much lower in nutrition.

Originally developed in the foothills of the Himalayas in northern India, Basmati rice is an aromatic white rice that is gaining in popularity. It is an excellent alternative for the 15-minute cook because it can be prepared in just that amount of time.

HOW TO COOK RICE
Using the appropriate amount of water or vegetable stock—2½ times the amount of brown rice or 2 times the amount of white rice—bring rice and liquid to a boil in a heavy saucepan. Cover and reduce heat to low. Simmer gently until all the water is absorbed: 20 minutes for white rice, 30 minutes for brown rice. Remove from heat and allow rice to stand, covered, for about 10 minutes. Fluff with a fork.

If you use rice regularly you might want to invest in an electric rice cooker. It will cook the rice perfectly without supervision.

Never stir rice while it is cooking. This will result in a sticky and gummy product. Removing the lid during cooking will also lower the quality of the rice.

1 cup uncooked brown rice yields about 2½ cups cooked rice

1 cup uncooked white rice yields about 3 cups cooked rice

Rice can be cooked ahead of time. Cooked rice will keep for 4 to 5 days in the refrigerator. It may also be kept frozen in bags or freezer containers for up to 2 months. Thawed rice does not stand well on its own, but it is acceptable in soups and well-seasoned skillet dishes.

The microwave effectively reheats precooked rice. Make sure the container is covered so that the steam will keep the rice moist. Rice may also be reheated in the top of a double boiler. Or place cooked rice in a heavy saucepan and sprinkle with 2 tablespoons water per cup of cooked rice. Cover tightly and heat for 5 to 10 minutes.

RICE VARIATIONS AND OTHER GRAINS
For a nut-flavored rice, try browning un-

cooked rice in hot butter, margarine, or oil in a heavy skillet. Stir constantly until lightly browned, then cook in liquid according to directions.

For a drier rice, toss rice lightly after cooking and place, uncovered, in a warm oven (200°–250° F.) for 5 minutes.

If you are in a hurry and do not have any precooked rice on hand, several grains other than rice are a pleasing and less time-consuming alternative. Try millet, bulgur wheat, or couscous.

Millet:
Use 2 cups liquid to 1 cup millet and cook for 25 to 30 minutes. For a nuttier flavor and slightly reduced cooking time, sauté millet in 1 tablespoon vegetable oil until it turns a golden brown. Then, add to cooking liquid, bring to a boil, and cook for about 20 minutes.

Bulgur wheat:
Use 1½ to 2 cups liquid to 1 cup bulgur wheat. Cook 20 minutes.

Couscous:
Combine equal quantities of couscous and hot liquid. Let stand, covered, until the liquid is completely absorbed, about 5 to 10 minutes.

PASTA

No longer thought of as Italian, pasta has very nearly replaced potatoes in the American diet. It is not high in calories: a 2-ounce serving has only 200 calories. And when combined with light, meatless sauces featuring fresh vegetables it is a wonderful choice for the health-conscious cook.

In its basic form, pasta is a mixture of durum wheat flour (semolina) and water. It is kneaded, shaped, and then dried or boiled fresh. Eggs are sometimes added to produce more delicate noodles. Spinach and tomatoes, and sometimes carrots or beets, can be included to add a bit of color.

Many stores now carry fresh pasta and enriched dried pasta in a wide variety of forms. Remember, fresh pasta keeps for only about 3 days in the refrigerator. It can, however, be frozen.

HOW TO COOK PASTA
For a main dish, allow 2 ounces dry pasta per serving or 3 ounces fresh pasta (1 cup cooked). Pasta "sizers" are nifty gadgets that will help you determine the correct amount of pasta to drop in your pot. If you do not have a pasta cooker, select a large pot that is deep rather than wide. It is not necessary to

cover the pot as the pasta cooks. Here is your guide to serving pasta for 4:

> *egg noodles: 6 cups*
> *bow ties: 4 cups*
> *elbow macaroni: 2 cups*
> *spirals: 3 cups*
> *spaghetti: 1¼-inch bunch*

Cook pasta in plenty of water: 2 quarts for 8 ounces is about right. Add the pasta in batches to water that has come to a boil. It is not necessary to add salt or oil to the cooking water; however, you can add 1 tablespoon olive or vegetable oil to the pasta as it is cooking to prevent it from sticking together. Do not overstir. Once, with a wooden fork, just as the pasta begins to soften is adequate. Do not stir again.

Cooking time depends on the type of pasta you have chosen. Homemade pasta is done in just *5 to 10 seconds*, dried homemade in just *5 minutes*, and dried commercial types in about *8 to 12 minutes*. Some Oriental noodles require only soaking for a few minutes in boiling water. Use package directions only as a guideline and rely on your own taste-testing to tell you when the pasta is done. If you pinch a pasta strand and see a white dot in the center, it is not cooked. Pasta is cooked perfectly when it is *al dente*, which means the strands are tender but still firm. Mushy pasta spoils the taste of almost any sauce, no matter how excellent.

Immediately drain well, because wet noodles will water down your sauces. My favorite pasta cooker has a stainless-steel liner that is pierced with holes. The pasta is easily removed from the pot and the liner acts as a colander, draining the noodles when they are done. There is no need to rinse pasta; however, if you plan to use it for a chilled salad, rinsing with cool water will help to speed up the process.

Many of my students ask if pasta can be cooked ahead of time. I feel that pasta is one of the few things you really should cook, drain, and sauce just before serving. But even though pasta is not a do-ahead item, it is still ideal for the 15-minute cook. All of the pasta toppings in this chapter can be made in 15 minutes or less *while the pasta is cooking.* Some of them do not even need to be cooked! If you time it just right, you should have pasta and topper ready at the same time. Remember, though, that even before readying your ingredients you should fill your pasta pot with water and bring it to a boil.

I have made suggestions for the type of pasta to be used with each recipe. Bear in mind that as a rule, shapes with ridges will trap sauces; they are ideal for light sauces. Rich sauces should be served with flat pastas or shapes that will trap less sauce.

LEGUMES

Although they are an incomplete protein, legumes (or beans) combine with many foods—milk, grains, seeds, nuts, or vegetables—to produce a complete protein. In addition to vegetable protein, legumes are good sources of carbohydrates, several B vitamins, and iron. Best of all, they are high in fiber and low in fat.

I have used canned beans for the recipes in this book because they are quick. Since they have added salt, drain and rinse them in cold water before using.

Dried beans will keep for several months and, once cooked, they can be stored for 1 to 2 days in the refrigerator. They may be cooked in large quantity when you have time and frozen for later use.

As a rule, *1 cup dry beans yields about 2½ cups cooked.* To cook dry beans, rinse first, removing stones, dirt, and any discolored beans. Cover beans with 3 to 4 times their volume in warm water and let them soak at least 3 to 4 hours or overnight in the refrigerator. Or, to speed up soaking time, place beans and water in a large saucepan, bring to a boil, and simmer for 5 to 10 minutes. Remove pan from the heat, cover tightly, and allow to soak for 2 to 3 hours.

After draining soaked beans, place them in a heavy-bottomed saucepan and cover with 1 quart fresh water for every 2 cups beans. Bring water to a boil, lower heat, and simmer for 1½ to 3 hours, depending on the type of bean: kidney beans require 1½ to 2 hours; chick peas and pinto beans 2 to 3 hours. Because lentils are soft-shelled and small, they require no soaking before cooking. Simply use 3 parts water to 1 part dry lentils and cook until tender, 30 to 60 minutes.

A slow cooker can also be used to cook legumes and has the advantage of requiring minimal attention from the cook. A pressure cooker can dramatically shorten cooking time.

OMELETS

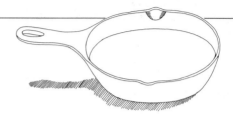

Omelets adapt themselves to breakfast, lunch, dinner, and even dessert. Leftovers make wonderful omelet fillings and, for variety, many sauces are ideal omelet toppings or fillings. Omelets can also be served without fillings when your time is limited. An elegant omelet can be made by simply adding chopped fresh herbs to the egg mixture.

You do not need a special omelet pan. If you have eggs on hand and a well-seasoned or non-stick skillet, you are ready to begin. Here's how:

HOW TO PREPARE A FRENCH OMELET
Begin with eggs at room temperature. Use 2 eggs per serving. For every 2 eggs add 1 tablespoon cold water to the omelet mixture. For a creamy, tender omelet, stir eggs and water with a fork just long enough to blend. It is not necessary to beat them. Heat margarine in the pan over high heat until it bubbles, then add eggs immediately. They should start to set around the edges as soon as they are poured into the pan. (For a more tender omelet, cook over moderate rather than high heat.) Stir egg mixture with a fork, tilting the pan occasionally so that uncooked portions can flow to the bottom. Stir until the fork leaves a clean path in the pan.

FLUFFY OMELETS
These light creations are made by beating the egg whites and yolks separately, cooking in a skillet, and completing the procedure in the oven. See page 122.

ADDING THE FILLING
Omelet fillings should be added to the pan *on top of the egg mixture* while it is still moist and creamy. If you are using a hot filling to topping, heat it separately before adding it to the omelet. Filling recipes and sauces are on pages 103–5. Other appropriate sauces appear on pages 24 and 106. Ideal leftovers include recipes on pages 96, 98, and 100.

A folded omelet takes practice. Place the filling along the center third of the omelet, slip a spatula under the third nearest the handle, and fold it gently over the filling. Slide the omelet on to a serving plate by sliding the outermost third on to the platter, then rolling the remainder over so the omelet lands seam side down.

OMELETS FOR A CROWD
This is not as hard as it sounds. For efficiency, begin with larger omelets. Roll them as they are removed from the pan and slice into single servings. Or keep the omelet flat as you slide it from the pan and top with filling and sauce. Cut it into wedges and serve.

CONDIMENTS

I like to keep this zesty mustard on hand because I find endless ways of using it in a variety of recipes. It is also a favorite of mine to share as a hostess gift.

ADVANCE PREPARATION
Pour into clean containers, cover, and refrigerate for up to 2 months.

HINT
◆ When using a double boiler, do not allow the simmering water to touch the bottom of the top pan.

MUSTARD

1 cup dry mustard powder
1 cup rice vinegar
3 eggs
1 cup sugar

In a small bowl, combine mustard and vinegar; whisk to remove lumps. Cover and allow to stand at room temperature overnight.

Pour mustard-vinegar mixture into a food processor or blender. Process with eggs and sugar until smooth.

Transfer mixture to the top of a double boiler. Cook, stirring constantly, over simmering water until the mixture thickens to pudding consistency, about 5 minutes.

makes about 2 cups

VARIATION
◆ substitute ¾ cup honey for sugar

Making your own mayonnaise is easy, cheaper than commercially prepared varieties, and free of preservatives. Most important, it is delicious!

Do not think of mayonnaise as just a dressing; served warm and seasoned with herbs and spices, it can also be a sauce over vegetables.

ADVANCE PREPARATION

The mayonnaise will keep for 3 weeks in the refrigerator. It will separate if frozen.

HINT

◆ Fresh steamed asparagus is delicious served with a mayonnaise sauce.

MAYONNAISE

2 eggs (at room temperature)
¼ cup rice wine vinegar or lemon juice
1 tablespoon honey
¼ teaspoon white pepper
dash of dry mustard
1½ cups safflower oil, at room temperature

In a blender or food processor, process ingredients except oil until smooth. Continue processing and add oil very slowly, until well mixed and thick.

makes 2 cups

VARIATIONS

◆ after mayonnaise is done, stir in 3 tablespoons finely chopped dill, tarragon, parsley, or watercress, or a combination. Thin with lemon juice or vinegar for a sauce consistency. Tomato paste or chili powder can also be added for variety.

◆ substitute 3 egg whites for 2 eggs; add a dash of turmeric for color

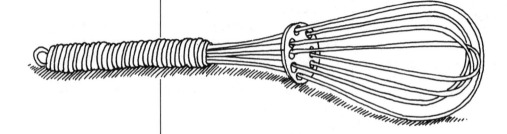

Chutney is an ideal accompaniment to curried main courses and it is an ingredient in several recipes in this book. It can be varied by substituting currants for raisins, or by adding ¼ cup chopped walnuts, pecans, or slivered almonds.

ADVANCE PREPARATION

Chutney will keep in the refrigerator for up to 2 weeks.

MIXED FRUIT CHUTNEY

8 dried apricot halves, chopped
½ apple, peeled and diced
¼ cup dark raisins
3 tablespoons water
3 tablespoons cider vinegar or rice vinegar
juice and rind of 1 lemon
2 tablespoons light brown sugar
½ teaspoon cinnamon
dash of freshly ground black pepper
2 pears, peeled, cored, and diced

In a medium-size saucepan, place ingredients except pears. Cover and cook over medium heat for about 10 minutes.
Add pears, cover, and cook for 5 minutes more.
Serve warm or refrigerate.
makes 2 cups

VARIATIONS
- ◆ to vary flavor, add ground allspice, cloves, or ginger
- ◆ substitute peaches for pears

PESTO

Pesto is traditionally a rich, green mash of fresh basil, pine nuts, garlic, olive oil, and Parmesan cheese put through a blender or ground with a mortar and pestle and served over warm pasta. This aromatic mixture is also an ingredient in appetizers, salads, and main dishes.

ADVANCE PREPARATION

◆ If not used immediately, spoon pesto into a jar and pour thin film of oil on top to prevent discoloration. Cover; refrigerate for up to 1 week. Bring to room temperature before tossing with pasta.

◆ To freeze, spoon pesto into foil-lined custard cups, cover tightly with foil, and freeze. When frozen, remove foil-wrapped pesto packets and place in a freezer bag for up to 2 months. To use, allow to thaw overnight; then use as fresh pesto.

HINTS

◆ Fresh herbs such as basil, dill, and chives will keep best if you wash them in slightly warm water. Shake and pat dry, and place in tightly closed jars in the refrigerator.

◆ Toss pesto with hot pasta and serve immediately or toss with hot pasta and chill to serve as a salad.

BASIC PESTO

2 cups fresh basil leaves
¼ cup pine nuts
2 cloves garlic
1 tablespoon olive oil

Place ingredients in bowl of a food processor fitted with steel blade. Process until smooth, using rubber scraper to push down the sides occasionally.

makes ½ cup

VARIATIONS

◆ add ¾ cup freshly grated Parmesan cheese
◆ substitute cream cheese, kefir cheese, or Neufchâtel cheese for oil
◆ substitute walnuts or hazelnuts for the pine nuts
◆ see Spinach-Parsley Pesto (p. 23) to make pesto without basil

DELICIOUS WAYS TO USE PESTO

◆ For an appetizer, stuff Pesto into hollowed cherry tomatoes, centers of raw mushrooms, or into celery sticks. Garnish with Parmesan cheese and freshly ground black pepper.

◆ For a raw vegetable dip to serve as an appetizer, stir 3 to 4 tablespoons of Pesto into ½ cup yogurt. Add Parmesan cheese and pepper to taste.

◆ Use Light Pesto Vinaigrette (p. 68) as a salad dressing or as a marinade for steamed and chilled vegetables.

◆ To make Pesto Herb Spread, in a food processor, combine 2 to 3 tablespoons Pesto with ½ cup softened unsalted margarine, 3 tablespoons grated Parmesan cheese, and a dash of lemon juice. Process until smooth. Pour into crock, cover, and chill. Serve as a spread for warm French bread to accompany soups, salads, and pasta dishes or serve on warm green beans, asparagus, potatoes, or spinach.

This recipe is for those times when you are in the mood for pesto, but fresh basil and pine nuts are unavailable. For variety, toss in steamed vegetables.

SPINACH-PARSLEY PESTO

8 ounces pasta (preferably thin whole wheat spaghetti)
2 cups chopped fresh spinach (stems removed), loosely packed (about ¼ pound)
1 cup fresh parsley leaves, loosely packed
½ cup grated Parmesan cheese
¼ cup chopped walnuts or pine nuts
2 cloves garlic
3 tablespoons chopped fresh basil or 1 tablespoon dried basil
1 tablespoon olive oil
¼ teaspoon black pepper

Garnish: *halved cherry tomatoes, walnut halves, or sweet red pepper rings, and additional Parmesan cheese, optional*

Bring a large pot of water to a boil; cook pasta until *al dente*.

Meanwhile, place remaining ingredients in a food processor and puree until smooth.

When pasta is cooked, drain well. Toss pesto with pasta. Top each serving with additional black pepper. Top with garnishes.

4 servings

SAUCES

A sauce can turn ordinary fare into something special. The following sauces are delicious on steamed vegetables, and can also be used to accompany a number of the recipes in the book.

This meatless tomato sauce can be used as an appetizer (served warm or chilled, or at room temperature), with slices of crusty French bread. It also serves as an omelet, pasta, or vegetable sauce.

ADVANCE PREPARATION

May be made up to 3 days in advance, refrigerated, and reheated.

HINT

◆ To make tomato sauce from tomato paste, add 2 cans water.

MARINARA SAUCE

1 tablespoon olive oil
1 small onion, chopped
2 cloves garlic, minced
1 medium-size carrot, shredded
1 stalk celery, chopped
¼ green bell pepper, chopped
1 6-ounce can tomato paste, preferably unsalted (⅔ cup)
1 8-ounce can tomato sauce, preferably unsalted (1 cup)
2 tablespoons chopped fresh parsley
1 teaspoon oregano
½ teaspoon thyme leaves
½ teaspoon basil
¼ teaspoon black pepper
dash of cayenne pepper
½ cup water

In a saucepan, heat olive oil. Stir in onion, garlic, carrot, celery, and green pepper as they are prepared; sauté until

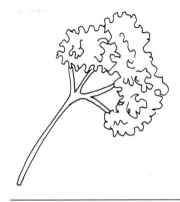

softened. Stir in remaining ingredients. Cover and simmer for 5 minutes.

makes 2 cups

VARIATIONS

♦ add chopped pimiento
♦ substitute a dash of dried crushed pepper for cayenne pepper
♦ add 2 cups finely diced ripe fresh tomatoes

♦

This versatile sauce is excellent on the Savory Nut Burgers (p. 116) and on the Vegetable Stir-Fry (p. 98). As a vegetable topper, I enjoy serving it on steamed green beans.

ADVANCE PREPARATION

May be made up to 3 days in advance, refrigerated, and reheated.

HINTS

♦ To peel a garlic clove easily, lay it on its side and swat it with the handle or side of a large chef's knife.

♦ To store garlic for months in the refrigerator, peel the cloves, place them in a small jar, cover with olive oil or safflower oil, and refrigerate. Use as needed; garlic will keep for 2 weeks. After you have used up the garlic, the flavorful oil can be used for sautéing or in salad dressing. (Commercially prepared garlic in oil can also be purchased at most supermarkets. Generally, it is crushed or chopped.)

GARLIC-TOMATO SAUCE

2 tablespoons margarine
1 small onion, chopped
2 cloves garlic, minced
1 tablespoon unbleached flour
1 teaspoon paprika
1 14½-ounce can whole tomatoes, drained, reserving juice
¼ teaspoon black pepper

In a medium-size saucepan, heat margarine. Sauté onion and garlic until onion is softened. Stir in flour and paprika until well blended; cook for 1 minute. Stir in reserved liquid from tomatoes. Cook, stirring constantly, until sauce is slightly thickened, about 2 minutes.

Add tomatoes and pepper; quarter tomatoes with kitchen shears. Stir until blended and heated through.

makes 2 cups

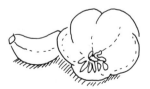

Made with ingredients you will have on hand, this sauce heads my list as a quick pasta or omelet topper.

ADVANCE PREPARATION

Not recommended; yogurt does not reheat well.

HINT

◆ Before heating yogurt, if possible, allow yogurt to reach room temperature to help prevent any separation.

Try this flavorful sauce as a topping for pasta or omelets.

ADVANCE PREPARATION

May be made up to 3 days in advance, refrigerated, and reheated.

TOMATO-YOGURT SAUCE

2 teaspoons safflower oil
2 cloves garlic, minced
1 6-ounce can unsalted tomato paste (²/₃ cup)
1 teaspoon dried oregano
¹/₂ teaspoon pepper
1 cup plain yogurt

Garnish: *fresh basil sprigs, optional*

In a small saucepan, heat the oil. Sauté garlic. Stir in tomato paste, oregano, and pepper. Cook, stirring, until sauce is heated through. Remove from heat and stir in yogurt; mix well. Place pan over low heat and stir just until mixture is warmed through; do not allow mixture to boil. Garnish with fresh basil sprig.
  makes 1¹/₃ cups

VARIATION

◆ substitute olive oil for safflower oil and basil for oregano

ZESTY TOMATO SAUCE

1 cup water or vegetable stock
1 6-ounce can tomato paste (²/₃ cup)
¹/₂ teaspoon paprika
¹/₂ teaspoon crushed red pepper
¹/₂ teaspoon black pepper
¹/₄ teaspoon ground coriander
¹/₄ teaspoon ground cumin

Place ingredients in a saucepan. Bring to a boil, reduce heat and simmer, uncovered, for about 10 minutes.
  makes 1¹/₄ cups

This unusual sauce is delicious on pasta and on the Vegetable Stir-Fry (p. 98), but my favorite use for it is on steamed vegetables, such as green beans or broccoli.

ADVANCE PREPARATION
May be made up to 2 days in advance and reheated.

HINT
◆ Tahini, composed of ground sesame seeds, is rich in calcium and is also an important source of protein, unsaturated oil, and fiber.

ORANGE-TAHINI SAUCE

1¼ cups orange juice
1 cup tahini
2 cloves garlic, minced
½ teaspoon ground coriander
dash of freshly ground black pepper

Garnish: *toasted sesame seeds*

Combine orange juice, tahini, and garlic in a food processor; puree.
Pour into saucepan, stir in coriander, and heat. Garnish with toasted sesame seeds.
makes 1½ cups

VARIATIONS
◆ add 1 tablespoon poppyseeds
◆ add 1 tablespoon soy sauce
◆ add a dash of cayenne pepper

This is my favorite sauce for the Vegetable Stir-Fry (p. 98) and for the Batter-Dipped Tofu appetizer (p. 34).

ADVANCE PREPARATION

May be made up to 2 days in advance and reheated.

HINTS

◆ Cornstarch and arrowroot give a clear quality to a soup or sauce while flour makes it opaque. Use slightly less arrowroot than cornstarch if you are making a substitution.

◆ To quickly mince fresh gingerroot, lay a slice of gingerroot flat on a cutting board, then bang it with the side of a cleaver or French chef's knife—presto! minced ginger. This method can also be used to mince fresh garlic.

GINGER SAUCE

6 tablespoons rice vinegar
6 tablespoons sugar
¾ cup plus 1 tablespoon water
2 tablespoons soy sauce
1 tablespoon cornstarch
1 tablespoon finely minced gingerroot

In a small saucepan, place vinegar, sugar, ¾ cup water, and soy sauce. Bring to a boil, reduce heat, and simmer, stirring occasionally, for 5 minutes.

Meanwhile, in a small bowl, combine cornstarch and 1 tablespoon water; stir into sauce. Cook mixture, stirring until clear and thickened.

Remove pan from heat; stir in ginger.
makes 1 cup

Poured over warm or chilled vegetables, such as steamed green beans or new potatoes, this sauce will add protein and variety to your meals.

ADVANCE PREPARATION

May be made in advance and kept in refrigerator for up to 3 days. Bring to room temperature if possible before using.

PEANUT SAUCE

4 tablespoons smooth peanut butter
½ cup milk
3 tablespoons plain yogurt
½ teaspoon oregano
½ teaspoon crushed red pepper

Garnish: *toasted sesame seeds, optional*

Mix together ingredients; garnish.
makes ¾ cup

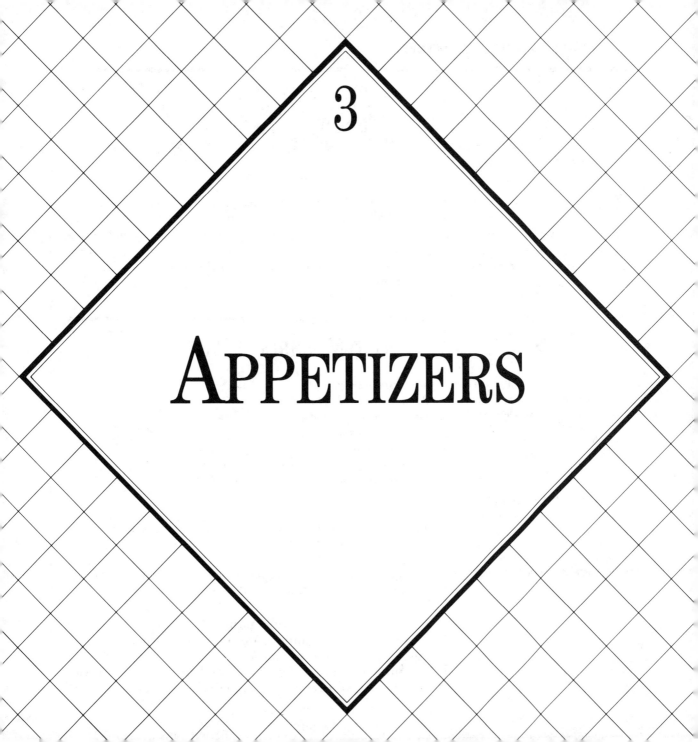

3

APPETIZERS

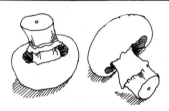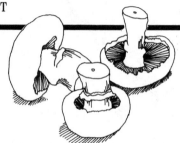

If you are having a party, forget the miniature hot dogs, the Swedish meatballs, the dips rich with sour cream. The light, tasty appetizers in this chapter rely on fresh vegetables, herbs, yogurt, light cheese, and interesting combinations. Each of them can be at least partially prepared ahead of time and then finished at the last minute and served. The best thing about them is they will satisfy your guests but leave them plenty of room for the main course.

People who do not like ordinary pâté seem to love this one. Vary the herbs and substitute the vegetables as you wish. Serve with water crackers, thick slices of crusty French bread, thin slices of whole wheat bread, or unsalted whole wheat crackers.

ADVANCE PREPARATION

The pâté may be served warm or at room temperature shortly after preparing, but it improves in flavor if it is refrigerated overnight. Bring to room temperature before serving. The pâté may also be frozen.

ALMOND-MUSHROOM PÂTÉ

2 tablespoons margarine
1 small onion, chopped (¼ cup)
1 clove garlic, minced
1½ cups sliced mushrooms (4 ounces)
½ teaspoon tarragon
1 cup blanched whole almonds (6 ounces)
1 tablespoon lemon juice
2 teaspoons soy sauce
dash of white pepper
2 tablespoons kefir cheese, Neufchâtel cheese, or cream cheese, optional

Garnish: *slivered or finely chopped almonds, fresh parsley sprigs, pimiento strips, or sweet red pepper strips, optional*

In a large skillet, melt margarine. Add onion, garlic, and mushrooms. Sauté until tender but not browned. Add tarragon; stir until it is softened.

Pour mixture into bowl of a food processor fitted with steel blade. Add remaining ingredients. Process until mix-

HINT

◆ Soy sauce is now readily available in a "lite" or "low sodium" variety which contains 40 percent less sodium than traditional soy sauce or tamari, but it still provides the same flavor. Remember it is still a sodium product to be avoided if you follow a strict sodium-restricted diet.

This is an easy appetizer to prepare in advance. The flavor improves if it is allowed to set in the refrigerator for a day or so. Serve it chilled as a dip for raw vegetables, or as a spread for Pita Crisps (p. 52) or sandwiches.

ADVANCE PREPARATION

May be made in advance and refrigerated for 1 to 2 days.

HINTS

◆ Smaller eggplants have thinner peels and a sweeter flavor. Select those with firm skin free of soft spots.
◆ Store sesame seeds in a cool, dark place in the refrigerator.

ture is smooth. Add cheese if you prefer a more spreadable consistency. Spoon into serving bowl. Top with garnish of your choice.

makes 1 ½ cups

VARIATIONS

◆ substitute other vegetables for the mushrooms; one of my favorites is broccoli
◆ substitute ½ teaspoon fennel for the tarragon and 1 cup whole pecans for the almonds
◆ vary the flavor by using other seasonings such as basil, oregano, dillweed, curry powder, or nutmeg
◆ add the kefir, Neufchâtel, or cream cheese if you prefer a more spreadable consistency

BABA GHANNOUJ
(EGGPLANT AND SESAME CREAM)

1 medium-size eggplant, peeled and cut into ½-inch cubes (about 3 cups)
¼ cup tahini
1 tablespoon lemon juice
1 clove garlic
¼ teaspoon black pepper
dash of ground cumin
2 tablespoons sesame seeds
2 tablespoons chopped fresh parsley

Garnish: *fresh parsley sprig, optional*

Steam eggplant until tender, about 8 minutes.

Place cooked eggplant in a food processor fitted with steel blade. Add tahini, lemon juice, and garlic. Puree.

Stir in remaining ingredients; spoon into serving bowl; garnish.

Serve warm or chill.

makes 2 cups

The popularity of this versatile appetizer is no surprise. I like it spread on cucumber rounds, garnished with halved cherry tomatoes and a sprig of parsley. It can also be used as a spread for bread or crackers, as a dip, or as a sandwich filling. Some brands of beans are moister than others, so the amount of lemon juice to be added may vary. Hummus should have a spreadable consistency.

ADVANCE PREPARATION

The flavor improves if the mixture is made 1 or 2 days in advance and refrigerated. Bring to room temperature, if possible, before serving.

HINTS

◆ Fresh herbs such as parsley will stay fresh longer if you refrigerate them in a covered jar with their stems in 1 inch of water. Or wrap the stem ends in a moist paper towel and seal them in a plastic bag in the refrigerator.

◆ Sesame seeds may be toasted in the oven on a baking sheet; however, I prefer toasting them in a dry non-stick skillet on the stove for about 10 minutes. Toss constantly and watch closely.

HUMMUS

1 tablespoon safflower oil
2 tablespoons chopped onion
1 clove garlic, minced
¼ cup minced fresh parsley
1 teaspoon basil
¼ teaspoon ground coriander
¼ teaspoon oregano
¼ teaspoon black pepper
dash of ground cumin
1 15-ounce can chick peas, drained and rinsed (1½ cups)
3 tablespoons lemon juice
2 tablespoons toasted sesame seeds

Garnish: *lemon wedges, cherry tomatoes, or fresh parsley sprigs, optional*

In a small skillet, heat oil; sauté onion and garlic until onion is softened. Add seasonings. Stir just long enough to soften parsley.

In a food processor, combine chick peas and lemon juice; process until smooth. Stir into onion and herb mixture; stir in sesame seeds. Spoon into serving bowl. Garnish with lemon wedges, cherry tomatoes, or parsley.
makes 1½ cups

VARIATIONS

◆ substitute 1 15-ounce can Great Northern beans for chick peas. Use only 2 tablespoons lemon juice since this is a moister bean.

◆ replace chick peas with ½ pound firm tofu (1 cup) and ½ cup tahini; use only 1 tablespoon lemon juice and add 1 tablespoon soy sauce

When friends drop in unexpectedly, this is a quick snack to prepare. Leftovers are ideal for lunch box sandwiches.

ADVANCE PREPARATION

This spread may be made in advance and refrigerated for 3 or 4 days.

CHEESY VEGETABLE SPREAD

1 cup shredded farmer cheese (4 ounces)
3 tablespoons plain yogurt
1 teaspoon lemon juice
1 teaspoon soy sauce
1/4 cup chopped apple
1/4 cup chopped carrot
2 tablespoons finely chopped celery
2 tablespoons chopped pecans
2 tablespoons currants
1 tablespoon toasted wheat germ
1/2 teaspoon curry powder

In a food processor fitted with a steel blade, process cheese, yogurt, lemon juice, and soy sauce until smooth.

Stir in remaining ingredients. Use as a spread on crackers, whole wheat bread, or Pita Crisps (p. 52), or stuffed into pita pockets.

makes 1 1/2 cups

VARIATIONS

- ◆ substitute shredded Cheddar for the farmer cheese
- ◆ mayonnaise may be substituted for the yogurt
- ◆ chop vegetables small, spread mixture on split pitas, and place under preheated broiler for about 3 minutes
- ◆ serve as an accompaniment to soups or salads
- ◆ use as a sandwich spread

Even "tofu skeptics" will enjoy this nutritious, high-protein appetizer.

ADVANCE PREPARATION

The sauce may be prepared in advance. Dry ingredients may be combined and set aside, as may be the egg-milk mixture. For best results, tofu must be sautéed just before serving.

HINTS

◆ For the recipes in this book, purchase toasted wheat germ; it keeps longer and has a nuttier flavor. Always refrigerate to prevent rancidity.

◆ Tofu is available in "firm" and "soft" varieties. Firm is the better choice when the tofu is to retain its shape; soft is preferable for using in blended desserts, dressings, and dips. Fresh tofu is always preferable to the canned variety.

BATTER-DIPPED TOFU

1 recipe Ginger Sauce (p. 28)
½ pound firm tofu
½ cup unbleached flour
2 tablespoons toasted wheat germ
½ teaspoon thyme
¼ teaspoon dill weed
¼ teaspoon garlic powder
¼ teaspoon paprika
¼ teaspoon black pepper
1 egg
1 tablespoon milk
3 drops hot pepper sauce
2 tablespoons safflower oil

Garnish: *curly lettuce leaves or large sprigs of fresh parsley, optional*

Prepare Ginger Sauce.

While it is simmering, cut tofu into 1-inch squares about ¼-inch thick. Set aside.

In a medium-size bowl, combine flour, wheat germ, and seasonings.

In a separate bowl, lightly beat egg. Add milk and hot pepper sauce.

In a large heavy skillet, heat oil. Piece by piece, dip tofu into flour, then in egg mixture, and again in flour. Sauté until lightly browned, about 3 minutes on each side.

Serve warm, arranged on a platter with cocktail forks and a bowl of sauce for dipping. Surround platter with curly lettuce leaves or large sprigs of parsley.

4 to 6 servings

VARIATIONS

◆ use egg white only
◆ the tofu squares may be cut larger and used as part of a

main course, topped with Vegetable Stir-Fry with Ginger Sauce (p. 98)
- ◆ substitute other sauces such as Zesty Tomato Sauce (p. 26), Tomato-Yogurt Sauce (p. 26), Sweet and Sour Sauce (p. 94), or Peanut Sauce (p. 28)

This is an ideal appetizer or snack for company when your time is short but you want to serve something unusual. If you do not have home-made chutney on hand, commercially prepared chutney will do.

ADVANCE PREPARATION

May be prepared several hours in advance; cover and refrigerate.

HINT

◆ Calorie comparisons per ounce: "lite" cream cheese: 60 calories; kefir cheese: 66 calories; Neufchâtel cheese: 80 calories; cream cheese: 100 calories.

CURRIED CHEESE SPREAD WITH CHUTNEY

1 cup shredded Cheddar cheese (4 ounces)
¾ cup kefir cheese (6 ounces)
2 teaspoons curry powder
1 cup Mixed Fruit Chutney (p. 21)
2 scallions, finely chopped

In a food processor fitted with steel blade, combine cheeses and curry powder. Puree until mixture is very smooth.

Spread cheese mixture in a 6-inch round serving dish. Spread with a layer of chutney. Sprinkle with chopped scallions.

Serve with crackers or Pita Crisps (p. 52).
makes 1 cup cheese spread plus chutney

VARIATIONS

- ◆ substitute cream cheese or Neufchâtel cheese for kefir cheese
- ◆ the pureed cheese mixture is delicious stuffed into hollowed-out cherry tomatoes or spread in celery sticks; garnish with parsley sprigs

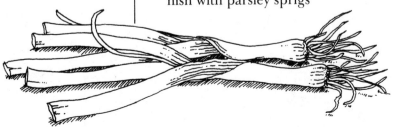

You will be surprised by how well peanut butter combines with vegetables; add a dash of crushed dried red pepper or a cayenne pepper if you like your food spicy. This dip is perfect with bland crackers or for a variety of fresh vegetables, such as carrots, broccoli, green or red peppers, or cauliflower.

ADVANCE PREPARATION

The flavors will blend and heighten if made in advance and refrigerated for a day or so.

HINT

◆ Use peanut butter that has no added fats, stabilizers, or sweeteners. If the oil rises to the top, simply stir it back in.

PEANUT CHILI DIP

⅓ cup peanut butter (smooth or crunchy)
3 tablespoons water
2 tablespoons soy sauce
2 tablespoons lemon juice
2 teaspoons honey
2 cloves garlic, finely minced
1 tablespoon chili powder
dash of crushed dried red pepper or cayenne pepper, optional

Garnish: *finely chopped peanuts and dash of paprika, optional*

Stir peanut butter and water into a paste and add other ingredients, mixing well. Spoon into serving bowl. Garnish with finely chopped peanuts and a sprinkling of paprika.
    makes ⅔ cup

NOTE

Add more water if your peanut butter is quite firm.

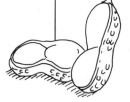

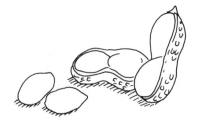

One of my favorite "skinny dips"—rich-tasting and flavorful without the calories of sour cream. Serve with your choice of fresh vegetables or Pita Crisps (p. 52).

ADVANCE PREPARATION

This dip can be served immediately, but chilling for several hours will allow the flavors to develop and blend.

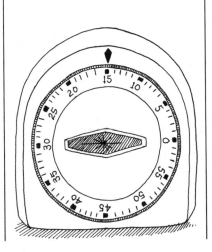

CURRIED YOGURT DIP

³⁄₄ cup plain yogurt
2 teaspoons curry powder
1 teaspoon lemon juice
¹⁄₂ teaspoon honey
¹⁄₄ teaspoon black pepper
few drops of hot pepper sauce

Garnish: *finely chopped almonds or walnuts, optional*

In a bowl, combine ingredients, stirring well. Spoon into serving bowl. If possible allow to set for 30 minutes at room temperature before serving. Garnish with a sprinkling of finely chopped almonds or walnuts.

makes 1 cup

OTHER APPETIZERS

The following appetizers can be adapted from other recipes in this book:

- ◆ *Almond Butter–Wheat Germ Sticks (p. 52)*
- ◆ *Guacamole Dip (p. 106)*
- ◆ *Italian Garden Frittata appetizer (p. 108)*
- ◆ *Marinara appetizer (p. 24)*
- ◆ *Nut Balls (p. 116)*
- ◆ *Pesto Dip (pp. 22–23)*
- ◆ *Pesto Stuffed Vegetables (pp. 22–23)*
- ◆ *Pita Crisps (p. 52)*
- ◆ *Stir-Fried Vegetables in Lettuce Cups (p. 98)*

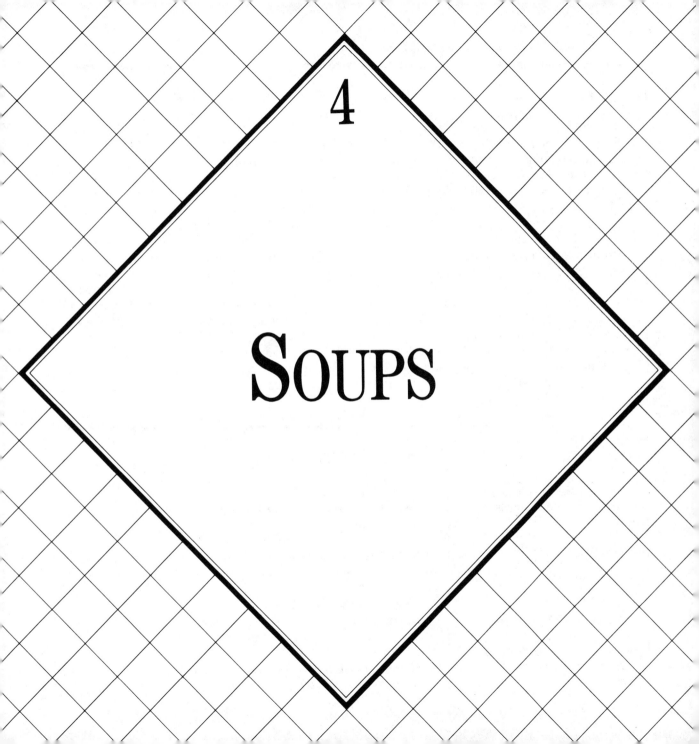

4

SOUPS

There is something special about homemade soup. I have never found a canned soup that can compare. In addition, the canned variety is often loaded with salt. But with a careful blend of herbs and spices, you can totally eliminate salt from your homemade soups.

I like to serve hot soups piping hot from a stainless steel-lined copper stock pot into heated bowls. If you have made the soup ahead of time, you can reheat just before serving.

Cold soups should be served icy cold, preferably in chilled bowls. If you have made the soup ahead of time, just remove from the refrigerator, garnish, and serve.

The garnish is important to presentation and taste. It can be as simple as a light sprinkling of chopped fresh herbs, finely chopped vegetables, grated cheese, sunflower seeds, nuts, or chopped egg. Or, if you have the time, prepare some Herbed Garlic Croutons (p. 51). I have suggested a garnish for each recipe, but I am sure you will delight in coming up with your own.

While many of my lighter soups make a delicious first course, others are hearty enough to stand on their own as a main course. Accompany them with Pita Crisps (p. 52), Almond Butter–Wheat Germ Sticks (p. 52), crusty bread, muffins, or whole wheat crackers, perhaps a cheese platter, and a tossed green salad.

This is an attractive soup, adaptable to many tasty variations. All provide a tempting mixture of flavors and textures, and the bonus is that the soup is elegant and low in calories. For a nuttier flavor, stir in 1 teaspoon of sesame oil just before serving.

ADVANCE PREPARATION

This soup will keep for several days in the refrigerator and reheats well, but take care not to overcook the vegetables.

ORIENTAL STEW

5 cups vegetable stock
1 small onion, thinly sliced, or 2 scallions, chopped
2 cloves garlic, minced
1 tablespoon minced gingerroot
1 to 2 tablespoons soy sauce
3 stalks bok choy, diagonally sliced, also shred leaves
1 cup broccoli florets
1 sweet red pepper, julienned
1 carrot, shredded
1 cup sliced mushrooms (3 ounces)
1/2 cup peas
2 ounces buckwheat noodles, broken into 1-inch pieces (1/2 cup)
1/2 pound firm tofu, cut into 1/2-inch cubes

HINTS

◆ Garlic is consumed in such small portions that its nutritive value is insignificant. Some cite it as an aid in reducing cholesterol, and it is often credited as being an aid to digestion.

◆ Blanch vegetables by placing them in a colander. Pour boiling water over them for just a few seconds, or immerse the colander in a pan of boiling water for a few seconds. Then pour on cold water. The color of the vegetables will brighten and the flavor will sweeten.

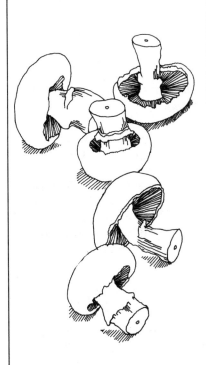

¼ cup watercress leaves
dash of white pepper

Garnish: *blanched peapods, thin scallion slices, celery leaves, toasted sesame seeds, finely shredded lettuce, or watercress leaves, optional*

Place ½ cup of the vegetable stock in a Dutch oven or 3½- to 5-quart saucepan and bring to a boil. Add onion, garlic, and ginger; simmer for 3 minutes. Stir in remaining stock and soy sauce. Cover pot and bring to a gentle boil. Add remaining ingredients as they are prepared. Test for doneness: noodles should be softened; vegetables should remain crisp-tender. Timing: 8 to 10 minutes. Top each serving with garnish.

6 servings

VARIATIONS

◆ substitute 1 cup cooked brown rice for the buckwheat noodles
◆ substitute or add other vegetables such as chopped green peppers, chopped water chestnuts, chopped jicama root, shredded spinach, chopped celery, or bamboo shoots
◆ to shorten preparation time, use only two vegetables: onion and peas
◆ for a "hotter" soup, substitute ½ to 1 teaspoon dry crushed pepper flakes for white pepper
◆ stir in 1 teaspoon toasted sesame oil or ½ teaspoon Chinese hot oil just before serving
◆ for additional protein and flavor, stir Egg Threads (see recipe below) into the soup just prior to serving

EGG THREADS

In a small skillet, heat a little margarine. When it begins to bubble, add 1 egg beaten with a little cold water. Tilt the pan so the yolk mixture coats it in a thin layer, the thinner the better. When the egg is lightly cooked, turn it out onto a cutting board. Slice it into very thin strips with a sharp knife.

about ⅓ cup

This is a meatless adaptation of one of our old favorites. In fall or winter, I use it often as a main-course soup with homemade corn bread and a crisp green salad.

ADVANCE PREPARATION

An ideal recipe to make several days in advance, if necessary. Flavors will blend; it reheats perfectly. Extra liquid may need to be added when reheating; use water, vegetable stock, or tomato juice.

HINTS

◆ ½ cup kidney beans contains 109 calories and 7 grams of protein.
◆ Beans are high in iron, potassium, calcium, vitamins A, B complex, and C, and are a good source of dietary fiber.
◆ Beans and corn bread will combine to form a complete protein.

MEATLESS MISSION CHILE

2 tablespoons safflower oil
1 clove garlic, minced
1 green bell pepper, chopped
1 stalk celery, chopped
1 small onion, chopped (¼ cup)
1 carrot, shredded
1 medium-size zucchini, shredded
1 18-ounce can tomatoes, with juice
1 15-ounce can kidney beans, drained and rinsed (1¾ cups)
1 8-ounce can tomato sauce (1 cup)
¼ cup water
1½ teaspoons chili powder, or to taste
¼ teaspoon hot pepper sauce, or to taste
1 teaspoon basil
1 teaspoon oregano
½ teaspoon black pepper

Garnish: *corn, chopped scallions, shredded Cheddar or Monterey jack cheese, or a combination, optional*

In a Dutch oven or 3½- to 5-quart saucepan, heat oil. Sauté garlic, green pepper, celery, onion, carrot, and zucchini until crisp-tender, about 3 minutes.

As the mixture cooks, stir in remaining ingredients. Bring to a boil over high heat, then reduce heat to medium. Cover and cook until heated through, about 5 minutes.

Garnish each serving with corn, scallions, or shredded cheese. If you wish, set under broiler to melt cheese.

4 servings

VARIATIONS

◆ add ½ cup whole raw cashews
◆ add ½ pound firm tofu, cut into ½-inch cubes
◆ add 1 cup cooked corn

This is a thick, robust soup that is a snap to prepare using a food processor. It is nourishing enough to be a light meal when served with slices of whole wheat bread and some fruit.

ADVANCE PREPARATION
Vegetables and stock may be pureed and refrigerated for up to 2 days. Heat mixture and add milk and nutmeg just before serving.

HINTS
◆ Unlike most vegetables, peas freeze reasonably well. Generally, I prefer the flavor of baby peas over standard-size ones.

◆ Skim milk can be used in this recipe. Of course, whole milk will result in a richer soup. For soups, I usually choose 2 percent milkfat. Skimmed or low-fat milk contains all the nutrients of whole milk without the fat and is more healthful because it is lower in cholesterol.

◆ Freshly ground whole nutmeg is much more aromatic than preground nutmeg. Many types of nutmeg graters are available in gourmet shops.

QUICK PEA SOUP

2 tablespoons margarine
2 stalks celery, finely chopped
2 cloves garlic, minced
1 medium-size onion, chopped (¹/₂ cup)
2 cups vegetable stock
1 16-ounce bag frozen peas, thawed (3 cups)
dash of white pepper
¹/₂ cup low-fat milk
dash of nutmeg (preferably freshly ground)

Garnish: *Herbed Garlic Croutons (p. 51), ¹/₄ cup chopped fresh parsley and 2 tablespoons chopped lemon peel, or grated Parmesan cheese, optional*

In a Dutch oven or 3¹/₂- to 5-quart saucepan, melt margarine. Add celery, garlic, and onion. Sauté until softened, about 5 minutes.

Add vegetable stock, peas, and white pepper. Over medium heat, cover and simmer for 5 minutes.

Transfer mixture to bowl of a food processor fitted with steel blade. Puree.

Return mixture to Dutch oven; add milk and nutmeg. Heat through, about 5 minutes, stirring constantly. Top each serving with your choice of garnish.

4 to 6 servings

VARIATION
◆ stir in 1 carrot, steamed and sliced, additional whole peas, or sautéed, sliced mushrooms

The main thickener in this soup, pureed potatoes and vegetables, eliminates the need for cream, butter, and flour frequently found in cream soups.

ADVANCE PREPARATION

This soup seems to improve in flavor if made in advance. When reheating, do not allow mixture to come to a boil. If you prefer, cook vegetables, puree, and refrigerate for up to 2 days. Heat mixture and add broccoli, milk, egg yolk, and soy sauce just before serving.

HINTS

◆ When adding egg yolks to a hot mixture, add small amounts of the mixture to the egg first, beating well. Cook over a low flame and do not allow mixture to come to a boil because it may curdle.

◆ Dissolving ¼ cup milk powder per cup of milk will provide added calcium and protein without altering the flavor.

PUREED VEGETABLE SOUP WITH BROCCOLI FLORETS

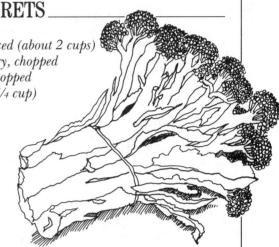

2 potatoes, peeled and diced (about 2 cups)
2 medium-size stalks celery, chopped
2 medium-size carrots, chopped
1 small onion, chopped (¼ cup)
1 clove garlic, minced
2 cups vegetable stock
¼ teaspoon black pepper
½ teaspoon thyme leaves
dash of nutmeg
3 cups broccoli florets
1 cup milk
1 egg yolk, lightly beaten
1 tablespoon soy sauce

Garnish: *minced fresh parsley, dash of paprika, minced fresh chives, grated cheese, sliced almonds, or finely diced sweet red peppers, optional*

In a Dutch oven or 3½- to 5-quart saucepan, place potatoes, celery, carrots, onion, garlic, stock, and seasonings. Bring to a boil, cover, lower heat, and simmer until vegetables are very tender, about 10 minutes. (The potatoes must be fully cooked to thicken the soup properly.)

While the soup is simmering, steam the broccoli florets.

When the simmered vegetables are tender, transfer with broth to a food processor; process until smooth.

Return pureed soup mixture to Dutch oven. Stir in broccoli florets. In a measuring cup, combine remaining ingredients. Add to soup and heat; do not allow mixture to boil. Top each serving with your choice of garnish.

4 servings

VARIATIONS

◆ for the steamed broccoli florets substitute 2 cups steamed,

...s steamed peas, or a com-

...owder for thyme and nut-
...slices or raisins
...cheese; melt into soup base
...ts; substitute a pinch of dry

...tock, or water if you prefer a

...SOUP

The ingredients are...
breeze to make, bu...
eaters will love it! ...
sliced cheese and ...
for a quick winter ...

...ed (½ cup)

...e (⅔ cup)

ADVANCE PRE...
This soup adapts p...
preparation and re...

...in
...r

HINTS
◆ If you chop onio...
bing your hands with lemon or celery, then washing, will remove the
odor.
◆ Slender, young carrots are sweeter
for eating fresh. Older ones are
thicker and tougher, ideal for soups.

...s or Herbed Garlic Croutons (p. 51),

In a Dutch oven or 3½- to 5-quart saucepan, heat oil. Stir in
carrots and onion; sauté until tender, about 5 minutes. Add
remaining ingredients, increase heat, and cover. When mixture reaches a boil, reduce heat to medium and simmer for
about 5 minutes. Garnish each serving with scallion curls or
Herbed Garlic Croutons (p. 51).

4 to 6 servings

VARIATIONS
◆ add ½ cup raisins. Cook soup until they are plumped and
tender
◆ add ½ cup chopped apple, simmering until tender
◆ add ½ cup cooked brown rice or ½ cup raw cashews

Ingredients from your pantry will create this hearty meal-in-a-bowl. The legumes (chick peas and kidney beans) and the grain (pasta) combine to form a well-balanced protein. The soup can be varied by changing the vegetables, beans, or type of pasta.

ADVANCE PREPARATION

May be made in advance and reheated.

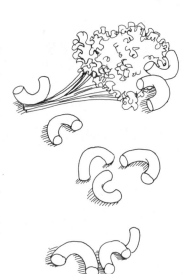

PASTA AND BEAN SOUP

½ cup elbow macaroni, small shells, or spaghetti broken into 1-inch lengths
2 tablespoons safflower oil
1 medium-size onion, chopped
1 clove garlic, minced
½ green bell pepper, chopped
3 cups vegetable stock or water
1 6-ounce can tomato paste (⅔ cup)
1 15-ounce can chick peas, drained and rinsed (1½ cups)
1 16-ounce can kidney beans, drained and rinsed (1¾ cups)
¾ teaspoon black pepper
½ teaspoon summer savory
½ teaspoon thyme leaves
dash of cayenne pepper

Garnish: *grated Parmesan cheese, optional*

Cook pasta in boiling water for about 6 minutes, until *al dente*.

While pasta is cooking, in a Dutch oven or 3½- to 5-quart saucepan, heat oil. Stir in onion, garlic, and green pepper; sauté until tender. Stir in remaining ingredients except macaroni. Cover and cook for 10 minutes. When pasta is done, drain well. Stir into other ingredients. Heat. Garnish each serving with grated Parmesan cheese.

4 to 6 servings

VARIATIONS

- ◆ substitute or add other vegetables such as chopped sweet red pepper, broccoli florets, or sliced mushrooms
- ◆ for Minestrone, substitute olive oil for safflower oil; add shredded carrot to sautéed vegetables; substitute 1 teaspoon basil and 1 teaspoon oregano for savory, thyme, and cayenne pepper
- ◆ to serve as a skillet main course, add only 1 cup vegetable stock, or use 3 cups vegetable stock and 1 cup pasta

I think chick peas have a unique flavor. Here they are used in a delicious main-course soup that supplies plenty of protein.

ADVANCE PREPARATION

May be made in advance and reheated.

HINTS

◆ Sesame paste and chick peas combine to form a complete protein.

◆ Chick peas are sometimes called garbanzo beans or ceci beans. They are found in the ethnic section of many grocery stores.

◆ Be sure to read the labels on canned goods; watch for salt-free or low-sodium varieties. Be aware that the words "no preservatives" do not mean a food is additive free; colorings and flavorings may still be added. Read the fine print!

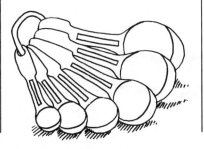

MOROCCAN CHICK PEA SOUP

2 tablespoons safflower oil
2 carrots, grated
2 cloves garlic, minced
1 medium-size onion, finely chopped (¹/₂ cup)
1 15-ounce can chick peas, drained and rinsed (1¹/₂ cups)
3 cups vegetable stock
¹/₃ cup tahini
2 tablespoons lemon juice
1 tablespoon chopped fresh parsley
³/₄ teaspoon ground cumin
¹/₂ teaspoon black pepper
¹/₂ teaspoon thyme leaves
¹/₄ teaspoon powdered turmeric
¹/₈ teaspoon cayenne pepper

Garnish: *toasted sesame seeds, minced scallions, finely chopped tomatoes, or Herbed Garlic Croutons (p. 51), optional*

In a Dutch oven or 3¹/₂- to 5-quart saucepan, heat oil. Add carrots, garlic, and onion; cook until tender. Set aside.

Meanwhile, in a food processor, puree chick peas, 1 cup of the vegetable stock, tahini, and lemon juice.

Stir pureed mixture into Dutch oven. Add remaining ingredients including remaining vegetable stock. Cover and cook for 5 minutes to heat through. Top each serving with garnish.

4 servings

VARIATIONS

◆ substitute olive oil for safflower oil

◆ add 1 medium-size sweet red pepper, finely chopped; sauté with carrots, garlic, and onion

This delicious and stoveless soup of Spanish origin is a welcome treat during the hot summer months. If you are planning to serve it immediately, start with chilled ingredients. Accompany it with a substantial salad such as the Couscous-Currant Salad with Lemon Dressing (p. 72) and a cheese platter.

ADVANCE PREPARATION

May be made in advance and refrigerated for several days. I love having it on hand for quick lunches and snacks.

HINT

◆ For even quicker Gazpacho, puree leftover mixed green and vegetable salad, dressing and all, with chilled tomato juice.

CHUNKY GARDEN GAZPACHO

1 15-ounce can tomato sauce (1 1/2 cups)
2 tablespoons olive oil
2 tablespoons red wine vinegar
1 tablespoon honey
1 medium-size tomato, cut into 1/2-inch cubes
1 medium-size green bell pepper, chopped
1 small sweet red pepper, chopped
1 stalk celery, chopped
1 clove garlic, finely minced
1 scallion, chopped
1/2 cucumber, seeded and chopped
1/2 teaspoon hot pepper sauce
1/2 teaspoon black pepper

Garnish: *Herbed Garlic Croutons (p. 51), dollop of plain yogurt topped with finely minced fresh chives, finely shredded lettuce, or minced fresh parsley, optional*

In a medium-size mixing bowl, combine tomato sauce, olive oil, vinegar, and honey. Stir in remaining ingredients. Serve chilled. Top each serving with garnish.
4 to 6 servings

VARIATIONS

◆ add 2 tablespoons chopped fresh mint leaves; omit hot pepper sauce
◆ for a thinner soup, stir in tomato juice or vegetable cocktail juice to desired consistency

This speedy chilled soup is one of my summer favorites when strawberries are at their ripest and sweetest. Since the soup is served cold, chilled bowls are a nice added touch and will help keep the soup cool on a warm day. If you are planning to serve it immediately, begin with chilled ingredients.

ADVANCE PREPARATION

If you begin with fresh ingredients, this soup may be made in advance and refrigerated for up to 2 days.

STRAWBERRY SOUP

1 cup plain yogurt
1 cup sliced fresh strawberries
2 tablespoons orange juice
1 tablespoon honey

Garnish: *fresh strawberry slices, fresh mint sprigs, or kiwi slices, optional*

In a food processor fitted with steel blade, blend ingredients. Serve chilled. Add garnish to each serving.
4 servings

VARIATIONS
♦ substitute white or red grape juice for orange juice
♦ substitute apple juice for orange juice
♦ serve in hollowed-out cantaloupe shells

Though I nearly always prefer fresh ingredients, this soup is actually best when made with frozen blueberries. Keep some on hand so you can surprise your family with this special soup.

ADVANCE PREPARATION

If you begin with fresh ingredients, this soup may be made in advance and refrigerated for up to 2 days.

BLUEBERRY SOUP

2 cups plain yogurt
2 cups orange juice
1 tablespoon honey
½ teaspoon cinnamon
1 cup frozen unsweetened blueberries, thawed

Garnish: *fresh mint sprigs, optional*

In a food processor fitted with steel blade, blend together yogurt, orange juice, honey, and cinnamon. Fold in blueberries.

Serve chilled in cold bowls. Garnish with fresh mint sprigs.

4 servings

VARIATION

◆ omit blueberries, add 1 ripe banana, and puree with other ingredients

AND WITH YOUR BEST SOUPS...

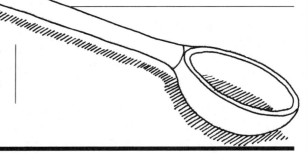

These soup or salad accompaniments do not take much time to prepare. In fact, you can make them right along with the main recipe. And they *are* worth the effort.

ADVANCE PREPARATION

Croutons may be prepared in advance. Store in a tin at room temperature for 1 to 2 days; some of their crispness will be lost if stored in a plastic container. They may be reheated and crisped by placing on a baking sheet in a 350° F. oven for 5 minutes.

HINTS

◆ Fresh herbs may be air-dried out of direct sun for 1 to 2 weeks, or may be dried in 100° F. oven for 24 to 48 hours.

◆ Dried herbs are more flavorful if they are finely crushed as you use them, either by rubbing between your fingers or by using a mortar and pestle.

HERBED GARLIC CROUTONS

4 tablespoons margarine, preferably unsalted
2 cloves garlic, minced
1/2 teaspoon basil
1/2 teaspoon oregano
2 cups whole wheat bread cubes, about 1/2 inch square

In a large skillet, heat margarine. Add seasonings. Cook for about 1 minute to soften. Stir in bread cubes and sauté until browned and crisp.

Scatter on tops of soups or salads just before serving.
makes 2 cups

VARIATIONS

◆ try other seasonings of your choice such as curry powder, chili powder, or thyme

◆ to bake, toss bread slices in melted margarine and oil; then cut into cubes. Spread on an ungreased baking sheet. Toast in preheated 400° F. oven for about 10 minutes, turning occasionally, until golden brown and crisp.

As an appetizer or as a crispy accompaniment to soups or salads, Pita Crisps will please your family and guests.

ADVANCE PREPARATION
Pita crisps are best when prepared just before serving.

PITA CRISPS

2 (6-inch-diameter) pita breads
2 teaspoons margarine
2 teaspoons oregano
4 tablespoons grated Parmesan cheese

Preheat broiler.

Split pitas horizontally into 2 rounds. Spread rough sides with margarine. Place on a cookie sheet.

In a small bowl, toss together oregano and Parmesan cheese. Sprinkle over margarine.

Cut each bread into wedges. Broil about 5 inches from heating element until crisp, about 2 minutes. Watch closely!
4 servings

VARIATIONS
- experiment with other herbs of your choice such as chives and parsley
- omit oregano and sprinkle with sesame seeds

These tasty bread strips are an ideal soup accompaniment or do-ahead appetizer; they also are my son's favorite lunch box surprise.

ADVANCE PREPARATION
Sticks may be prepared in advance. To retain crispness, store in an airtight container and refrigerate.

ALMOND BUTTER–WHEAT GERM STICKS

4 slices firm whole wheat bread
⅓ cup blanched or roasted almond butter
2 tablespoons safflower oil
¼ cup toasted wheat germ

Preheat oven to 350° F.

Trim crusts from bread slices. Cut each slice into 4 strips. Place strips on a baking sheet.

Toast bread strips in oven for 5 minutes. Turn them and

HINT
◆ Almond butter, a product similar to peanut butter, is made from pureed almonds; salt is often added.

toast for another 5 minutes, or until lightly toasted and crispy.

Meanwhile, in a small saucepan, heat almond butter and oil, stirring occasionally, until thinned and smooth.

Into a shallow dish, pour toasted wheat germ.

Dip both sides of each toasted bread strip into warm almond butter; then press each side in wheat germ. Place on baking sheet to dry for a few minutes.

makes 16 sticks

VARIATIONS

◆ substitute peanut butter or cashew butter for the almond butter or use a combination
◆ add 1 tablespoon honey when heating the almond butter or peanut butter
◆ heat extra almond butter or peanut butter; add a dash of honey and carob powder, some sesame seeds or sunflower seeds—Presto! Carob fudge! Spread in a small pan or form into small balls and refrigerate.

NOTES

◆ Dry bread crusts and crumble to use as bread crumbs in other recipes.
◆ Amount of oil needed may vary according to brand of almond, peanut, or cashew butter used.

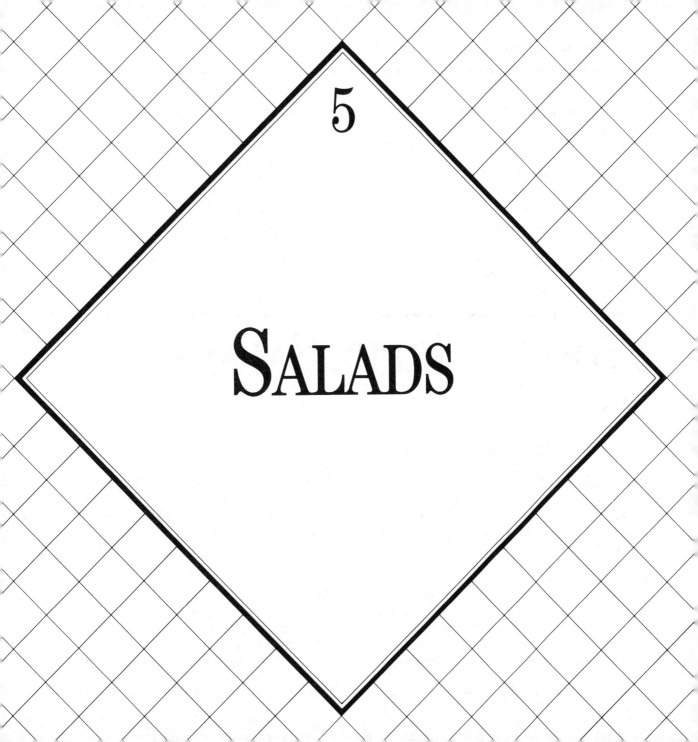

5

SALADS

Salads can be either the star or the supporting player of a meal. Prepared carefully and arranged artfully, salads can add texture, color, coolness, and even an ethnic touch. Or they can make a beautiful, refreshing main course to please the heartiest appetite.

When using a salad to accompany a main course that is spicy and hot, choose one that is cool and green. If the main course is subtle, the salad should be bold, crunchy, and tart. If the main course is unusual or exotic, the salad should be reserved and not compete for attention.

One of the nicest things about salads is the diversity of ingredients that can be used to make them. Always start with the freshest, highest-quality fruits and vegetables.

Since every meal should include a protein source, many of my salads contain seeds, nuts, tofu, and cheese. In fact, many of them are substantial enough to stand on their own as a main course.

Tossed Green Salads

A simple tossed salad is often an ideal quick-to-prepare addition to a 15-minute main course. Or, with more time and a wider array of ingredients, the salad can be turned into a healthful main course itself. For an informal lunch or dinner, try a make-it-yourself salad bar accompanied by homemade dressing, soup, and a selection of breads. As an added touch, toss salads in a chilled bowl and serve on chilled plates or bowls.

The success of a green salad depends on crisp fresh greens. Wash the greens well under cold running water. Drain and dry them thoroughly in a salad spinner or on toweling. Store in an airtight container in the refrigerator; or, if the greens are to be used soon, roll in a towel and refrigerate. To avoid brown edges, always tear the lettuce leaves by hand. As a time saver, chop vegetables when time permits; refrigerate in airtight containers for 2 to 3 days.

Although some salads are classics, there are really no rules for making a good salad combination. Salad ingredients can be much more than just lettuce and tomatoes. Here are some suggestions for adding variety to your salads. I have also included recipes for several of my favorite healthful dressings.

DRESSING SALADS
- Dress bean and grain salads as soon as they are prepared.
- Leafy green salads will wilt and lose their crispness if dressed more than just a few minutes before they are eaten. Add just enough dressing to coat the ingredients.

THE 15-MINUTE VEGETARIAN SALAD BOWL

Greens

lettuce: Bibb,   Chinese cabbage
  Boston,   endive
  celery leaves,   escarole
  iceberg,   parsley
  Napa cabbage,   spinach
  red leaf, romaine   watercress

Low-Calorie Additions

alfalfa sprouts   celery
asparagus   cucumbers
bean sprouts   green bell peppers
beets   green beans:
broccoli florets   cooked or raw
cabbage   jicama root
carrots   leeks
cauliflower florets   mushrooms

onions   summer squash
peapods   sweet red pepper
peas   tomatoes
potatoes   water chestnuts
radishes   zucchini
scallions

Protein Additions

beans: chick peas,   eggs: hard-cooked or
  kidney beans,   Egg Threads (p. 41)
  lentils   nuts
cheese   seeds

Miscellaneous Additions

fruit: apples,   rice, barley,
  grapes, orange   bulgur wheat
  sections, raisins, Herbed Garlic
  strawberries   Croutons (p. 51)
grains: couscous,   pasta

This is my favorite salad dressing to keep on hand for serving on green salads or fruit. I especially like it on a salad of lettuce, mandarin oranges, celery, raisins, and slivered almonds.

ADVANCE PREPARATION

This dressing may be made in advance and refrigerated for up to 2 weeks. Shake or stir before using.

HINT

◆ In recipes calling for oil and honey, measure the oil first. Then use the same measuring cup, without washing, for the honey. It will easily slide out of the cup when you pour.

HONEY-POPPYSEED DRESSING

⅓ cup rice vinegar
⅓ cup safflower oil
⅓ cup honey
1 tablespoon poppyseeds
¼ teaspoon black pepper

Whisk together ingredients. Stir or shake well before serving.
   makes 1 cup

I especially like this dressing on a mixture of lettuce, chopped scallions, bean sprouts, alfalfa sprouts, slivered almonds, mandarin oranges, peapods, chopped jicama, and chopped celery.

ADVANCE PREPARATION

This dressing may be made in advance and refrigerated for up to 1 week.

HINT

◆ Cider vinegar and white vinegar are harsher in flavor than wine vinegar. I think rice vinegar is the softest and most pleasant.

This recipe has been adapted from my favorite salad dressing served at a restaurant in Naples, Florida. I have eliminated the oil without sacrificing flavor.

ADVANCE PREPARATION

This dressing may be made in advance and refrigerated for up to 2 weeks.

HINT

◆ Store honey at room temperature. If it crystallizes, place the jar in hot water to dissolve the crystals.

SESAME SOY DRESSING

⅓ cup rice vinegar
3 tablespoons sesame oil, preferably toasted sesame oil
2 tablespoons soy sauce
2 teaspoons minced gingerroot
2 teaspoons sesame seeds, toasted or untoasted
3 teaspoons sugar
dash of white pepper

Whisk together ingredients, stirring until sugar is dissolved. Stir or shake before using.
makes ½ cup

TANGY HONEY-MUSTARD DRESSING

2 tablespoons mayonnaise
2 tablespoons rice vinegar
1 tablespoon lemon juice
1 teaspoon Dijon mustard
1 teaspoon honey
1 clove garlic, minced
dash of white pepper
few drops of hot pepper sauce
1 scallion, finely chopped
1 tablespoon finely minced fresh parsley

In a food processor, blend together all but last 2 ingredients. Add scallion and parsley and process again. Stir or shake dressing before using.
makes ½ cup

This is a basic vinaigrette dressing that can be varied by using your choice of herbs.

ADVANCE PREPARATION

This dressing may be made in advance and refrigerated for up to 1 week.

HINTS

◆ Dijon mustard is now available in unsalted form. Or if you prefer, make your own spicy mustard from the recipe on page 19.

◆ If you use a garlic press, wash it immediately after each use; it will be very difficult to clean if the remains of the garlic dry in it. Clean out stubborn strands of garlic with a toothpick.

This low-calorie dressing is excellent on tossed green salads, sliced tomatoes, or mixed fruit salads.

ADVANCE PREPARATION

If the yogurt is fresh, this dressing will keep in the refrigerator for up to 1 week.

VINAIGRETTE DRESSING

4 tablespoons lemon juice
4 tablespoons red wine vinegar
2 tablespoons olive oil or safflower oil
1 tablespoon Dijon mustard
1 tablespoon basil
1 teaspoon black pepper
½ teaspoon oregano
1 clove garlic, minced

Stir together ingredients. Stir or shake before using.
  makes ½ cup

VARIATIONS

◆ for a lower calorie dressing, oil may be omitted
◆ experiment by adding other herbs such as marjoram, tarragon, parsley, paprika, celery seed, coriander, chives, or thyme
◆ use other vinegars such as rice, white, cider, or herb vinegar
◆ for sweetness, add a dash of honey

APPLE SALAD DRESSING

½ cup plain yogurt
¼ cup apple juice concentrate (undiluted)
1 tablespoon lemon juice
1 teaspoon honey
½ teaspoon celery seed
¼ teaspoon black pepper

In a small bowl, whisk together ingredients. Stir well before using.
  makes 1 cup

A variation on a traditional salad dressing—ideal for summer. Terrific on a lettuce salad topped with grated carrots and sunflower seeds.

ADVANCE PREPARATION

For freshest flavor, make just before serving; but dressing may be made up to 2 days in advance and refrigerated.

SUMMER PEACH VINAIGRETTE

1 peach, peeled and seeded
2 tablespoons lemon juice
¼ cup safflower oil
2 tablespoons rice vinegar
dash of freshly ground black pepper

In a food processor, puree peach with lemon juice. Add other ingredients and process until smooth. Shake or stir before using.
makes ½ cup

VARIATIONS
- add a dash of honey or sugar
- substitute a nectarine for the peach
- for Strawberry Vinaigrette, substitute ½ cup sliced strawberries for the peach, 1 tablespoon orange juice concentrate for lemon juice, red wine vinegar for rice vinegar, and 1 teaspoon sugar for pepper

Chutney Dressing is an ideal use for extra chutney. I like it on tossed green salads or mixed fruit salads.

ADVANCE PREPARATION

This dressing may be made in advance and refrigerated for up to 1 week, providing chutney is fresh. Shake or stir before using.

CHUTNEY DRESSING

½ cup Mixed Fruit Chutney (p. 21)
⅓ cup safflower oil
¼ cup lemon juice
2 tablespoons water
¼ teaspoon curry powder

In a food processor, blend together ingredients.
makes 1 cup

This is one of the most attractive salads. In fact, it warrants the purchase of a deep clear glass salad bowl to do it justice!

ADVANCE PREPARATION

Dressing may be made in advance and refrigerated. Spinach may be cleaned in advance, rolled in clean towels, and refrigerated. Clean strawberries and toss salad just before serving.

HINTS

◆ If you purchase spinach in plastic bags, remove the spinach from the bag and refrigerate it uncovered or wrapped in a towel. Moisture in plastic bags can cause spinach to spoil quickly.

◆ To quickly remove spinach stems, fold the leaf in half, pull and zip off the stem.

SPINACH AND STRAWBERRY SALAD WITH PEPPER VINAIGRETTE

PEPPER VINAIGRETTE
2 tablespoons safflower oil
1 tablespoon cider vinegar
2 teaspoons honey
¼ teaspoon black pepper
dash of hot pepper sauce
dash of cayenne pepper

SALAD
6 ounces fresh spinach, stems removed and leaves torn (3 cups)
12 strawberries, halved

Garnish: *toasted sesame seeds, optional*

In a small bowl, combine dressing ingredients.

In a salad bowl, toss spinach with dressing. Toss in strawberries. Garnish with toasted sesame seeds.

4 servings

VARIATIONS
◆ add halved seedless green grapes or substitute them for strawberries
◆ add ¼ cup slivered almonds

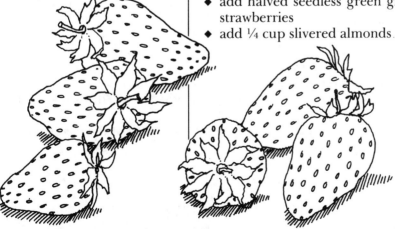

This pleasant mixture of flavors and textures goes well with tomato-based soups such as Winter Carrot Soup (p. 45). Serve with warm whole wheat rolls and cheese for a simple meal.

ADVANCE PREPARATION

Dressing may be made in advance and refrigerated. Spinach may be cleaned in advance, rolled in clean towels, and refrigerated. Chop fruit and toss salad just before serving.

HINTS

◆ Yogurt provides vitamin D, the B complex vitamins, protein, and calcium.

◆ Walnuts, like most nuts, will keep for 1 month at room temperature, in the refrigerator for about 3 months, and for 6 to 12 months in the freezer. It is not necessary to thaw them before using.

WINTER FRUIT SALAD WITH CURRIED YOGURT DRESSING

SALAD

8 ounces spinach leaves, stems removed and leaves torn (4 cups)
1 apple, cut into ½-inch cubes
1 pear, cut into ½-inch cubes
1 stalk celery, coarsely chopped
1 cup seedless green grapes
1 cup bean sprouts

CURRIED YOGURT DRESSING

⅓ cup plain yogurt
2 tablespoons lemon juice
1 tablespoon honey
½ teaspoon curry powder, or more to taste
dash of ground cinnamon

Garnish: *sesame seeds, raw sunflower seeds, or chopped walnuts, optional*

In a salad bowl, toss together salad ingredients.

In a small mixing bowl, combine dressing ingredients, mixing well. Spoon over the salad and toss. Top with garnish and serve immediately.

4 servings

VARIATIONS

◆ substitute lettuce for spinach leaves
◆ toss in ½ cup chopped walnuts, chopped pecans, or raw sunflower seeds
◆ substitute mayonnaise for part or all of the yogurt in the dressing

This light and flavorful salad is perfect for a patio or rooftop party because it goes well with a variety of other foods and can be made ahead.

ADVANCE PREPARATION

The salad and dressing may be tossed together several hours before serving.

HINT

◆ Sprouting is the only process used in food preparation that increases a food's nutritional value. Sprouts can be the freshest vegetable you eat because they are still growing when you eat them. Even fresh vegetables lose up to 25 percent of their vitamins just 30 minutes after being picked. Avoid using canned bean sprouts; they lack the color, texture, and nutrition of fresh sprouts.

FRUIT AND SPROUT SALAD WITH GINGERED YOGURT DRESSING

SALAD

1 cup fresh bean sprouts
1 8-ounce can mandarin orange segments, drained, or 1 fresh orange, sectioned
1 8-ounce can pineapple tidbits in own juice, drained
1 8-ounce can sliced water chestnuts, drained
1 stalk celery, diced

GINGERED YOGURT DRESSING

1/4 cup plain yogurt or mayonnaise
1 teaspoon honey
1/2 teaspoon soy sauce
1 teaspoon curry powder
1/2 teaspoon ginger powder

crisp greens

Garnish: sunflower seeds, sesame seeds, or chopped pecans, optional

In a large bowl, toss together salad ingredients.
    In a separate small bowl, mix dressing ingredients. Pour over salad mixture and toss.
    Serve on beds of crisp greens. Top with garnish.
    4 servings

Because of the peanut butter and generous use of vegetables, this is a filling dish that makes an excellent and out-of-the-ordinary main-course salad.

ADVANCE PREPARATION

Both salad ingredients and dressing may be prepared in advance and refrigerated. For best quality, toss together just before serving.

HINTS

◆ Tofu, peanuts, and sesame seeds complement one another to form a high-quality complete protein.
◆ To cook bean thread, immerse it in boiling water for about 10 minutes to soften. Drain, rinse with cool water, and cut into 3-inch strands.

INDONESIAN VEGETABLE SALAD

1 cup cubed, firm tofu (½-inch cubes)
2 stalks celery, cut into julienne strips
2 carrots, shredded
2 Italian plum tomatoes, cut into thin wedges
½ cucumber, thinly sliced
1 cup fresh bean sprouts
1 cup broccoli florets
1 cup cauliflower florets
½ cup Szechwan Peanut Dressing (p. 89)

Garnish: *raisins, toasted sesame seeds, fresh watercress sprigs, or unsalted peanuts, optional*

In a large bowl, gently toss together salad ingredients.
In a small bowl, combine dressing ingredients. Pour over salad and toss again. Top with garnish.
4 to 6 servings

VARIATIONS

◆ add or substitute other vegetables such as steamed green beans, fresh spinach, blanched peapods, mushrooms, jicama, or boiled new potatoes
◆ add Egg Threads (p. 41) or hard-cooked eggs, cut into wedges
◆ spread the salad over a bed of cooked bean thread; serve with Sesame Soy Dressing (p. 58)

This salad is an ideal accompaniment to a spicy main course such as the Vegetable Curry on page 96.

ADVANCE PREPARATION

May be prepared 1 day in advance; if allowed to set, flavors will blend.

HINTS

◆ Coriander is also called Chinese parsley or cilantro.
◆ For variety, try English (or European) cucumbers. They have fewer seeds and are thinner and more tender; their unwaxed skins eliminate the need for peeling.

THAI CUCUMBER SALAD

4 tablespoons white vinegar
4 tablespoons sugar
1 large cucumber, very thinly sliced
1 small shallot, very thinly sliced
1 tablespoon finely chopped and seeded red hot chili pepper

Garnish: *chopped fresh coriander or thinly sliced radishes, optional*

In a small saucepan, combine vinegar and sugar; bring to a boil. Cook, stirring occasionally, just until the sugar dissolves. Remove from heat and allow to cool.

In a medium-size bowl, toss together cucumber, shallot, and pepper. Pour sauce over cucumber mixture and stir. Top with garnish. Refrigerate.

4 to 6 servings

NOTE

When planning your menu, prepare this salad first to allow time for cooling. Serve with a slotted spoon; leftover dressing can be reused.

VARIATIONS

◆ add thinly sliced carrots, tomatoes, or green bell pepper
◆ for a milder flavor, substitute green chili pepper or jalapeño for red hot chili pepper

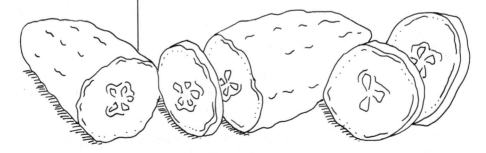

The seasonings in this salad are intriguing. It is not the potato salad that Mom used to make.

ADVANCE PREPARATION

To serve warm, prepare and serve immediately. To serve chilled, prepare earlier in the day and refrigerate.

HINTS

◆ When boiling potatoes, cut into cubes of uniform size so they will cook at the same rate.

◆ It is not necessary to peel potatoes for potato salad; potatoes eaten with their skins have more nutrients. Scrub them well before cooking; many potatoes are sprayed with chemicals to keep their "eyes" from sprouting.

FRENCH POTATO SALAD WITH SAVORY VINAIGRETTE

SALAD
1½ pounds new potatoes (about 12)
1 bay leaf
2 tablespoons chopped onion
½ teaspoon black pepper

SAVORY VINAIGRETTE
2 tablespoons safflower oil or olive oil
2 tablespoons white wine vinegar
1 tablespoon chopped fresh parsley
1 clove garlic, finely minced
1 teaspoon summer savory
½ teaspoon black pepper
¼ teaspoon dry mustard

Garnish: *cherry tomato slices, or grated Cheddar cheese mixed with chopped fresh parsley, optional*

Fill half a large pot with water; over high heat, bring to a boil. Meanwhile, scrub potatoes and cut into large cubes or thick slices. Add to water with bay leaf, onion, and pepper. Simmer potatoes until just tender, about 8 minutes. Remove bay leaf and drain.

While potatoes are cooking, mix together dressing ingredients.

In a large bowl, toss dressing with warm potatoes. Top with garnish and serve immediately.

4 to 6 servings

VARIATIONS

◆ add other vegetables such as grated carrots or steamed cut green beans
◆ place in an oven-proof bowl, top with grated Cheddar cheese, and broil until cheese is melted

Though this is not an authentic Oriental dish, the combination of flavors and textures is intriguing.

ADVANCE PREPARATION

To serve warm, prepare and serve immediately. To serve chilled, prepare earlier in the day and refrigerate.

HINTS

◆ Potatoes are best stored in a cool, dark, well-ventilated place. The ideal temperature is 40° to 50° F. Potatoes should not be stored in the refrigerator, where the starch will begin to convert to sugar.

◆ Potatoes are an excellent source of vitamin C, several B vitamins, and fiber. They are one of the best sources of complex carbohydrates.

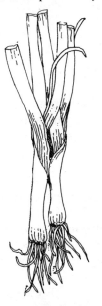

ORIENTAL POTATO SALAD WITH SOY DRESSING

SALAD
1 tablespoon honey
1½ pounds new potatoes (about 12)
1 cup fresh bean sprouts
1 cup sliced mushrooms
1 stalk celery, diced
1 scallion, chopped
¼ cup chopped fresh parsley

SOY DRESSING
¼ cup safflower oil
2 tablespoons rice vinegar
1 tablespoon soy sauce
1 tablespoon water
¼ teaspoon ginger powder
dash of garlic powder

Garnish: *toasted sesame seeds and fresh watercress leaves, optional*

Fill half a large pot with water; add honey. Place over high heat and bring to a boil. Meanwhile, scrub potatoes and cut into large cubes or thick slices. Simmer potatoes until just tender, about 8 minutes. Drain.

While potatoes are cooking, prepare other salad ingredients. Set aside.

In a small bowl, whisk together dressing ingredients.

In a large bowl, toss vegetables with warm potatoes. Pour on dressing and toss again. Top with garnishes and serve warm.

4 to 6 servings

VARIATION
◆ substitute or add other vegetables such as peas

This is an out-of-the-ordinary potato salad, It is attractive, tasty, and satisfying.

ADVANCE PREPARATION

To serve warm, prepare dressing and salad just before serving. To serve at room temperature, make up to 1 hour before serving. If made further in advance, the salad can be refrigerated to chill.

HINTS

◆ If time allows, for best vitamin retention, cook potatoes whole, then cut into cubes.
◆ Potato salad should be made with new (or small boiling) potatoes. Mature baking potatoes break apart too easily and absorb too much of the dressing.

POTATO SALAD WITH LIGHT PESTO VINAIGRETTE

SALAD
1½ pounds new potatoes (about 12)
1 carrot, shredded
½ green bell pepper, chopped
1 scallion, chopped

LIGHT PESTO VINAIGRETTE
3 tablespoons rice vinegar
2 tablespoons Pesto (p. 22)
2 tablespoons safflower oil
1 tablespoon water
dash of freshly ground black pepper

Garnish: *sprinkling of Parmesan cheese, optional*

Half fill a large pot with water; place over high heat and bring to a boil. Meanwhile, scrub potatoes and cut into large cubes or thick slices. Simmer potatoes until just tender, about 8 minutes. Drain.

While potatoes are cooking, prepare other salad ingredients. Set aside.

Place dressing ingredients in bowl of a food processor; process until blended.

In a large bowl, toss vegetables with warm potatoes. Pour on dressing and toss again. Garnish with cheese and serve warm.

4 to 6 servings

VARIATIONS
◆ add other vegetables; steamed green beans are especially good. You may need more dressing.
◆ Light Pesto Vinaigrette is also delicious as a marinade for sliced tomatoes, sliced mushrooms, steamed asparagus, or steamed green beans, or as a dressing on green salads.

This crunchy, colorful salad is perfect for those occasions when you want a salad that can be prepared ahead and will not wilt or spoil. It is a nice accompaniment to the Guacamole Omelet with Tomato Hot Sauce (p. 106).

ADVANCE PREPARATION

Salad may be served immediately or may be made 1 day in advance and refrigerated.

HINT

◆ Fresh basil leaves should be a vivid green and not wilted or marked with dark spots.

BASIL BEAN SALAD

SALAD
1 16-ounce can Great Northern beans, drained and rinsed (1¾ cups)
1 cucumber, chopped
1 sweet red pepper, chopped

DRESSING
2 tablespoons safflower oil
2 tablespoons cider vinegar
1 tablespoon lemon juice
2 tablespoons chopped fresh basil or 2 teaspoons dry basil
1 tablespoon minced fresh parsley
¼ teaspoon black pepper

lettuce leaves

Garnish: chopped scallions, optional

In a mixing bowl, combine beans, cucumber, and red pepper.

In a small bowl or measuring cup, combine dressing ingredients. Pour over bean mixture and toss.

Using a slotted spoon, arrange on lettuce leaves on individual chilled salad plates. Garnish with chopped scallions.

4 to 6 servings

VARIATION
◆ add chopped red onion to the salad

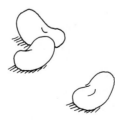

Salads are a terrific way to use leftover grains. Brown rice is my favorite, but other grains such as bulgur wheat or couscous also work well. For a light summer supper or luncheon, serve with soup, muffins, and a fruit dessert.

ADVANCE PREPARATION

The salad may be made early on the day it is to be served. If kept longer, the dressing tends to be absorbed into the grain.

HINT

◆ Arugula, also called Roquette or Rocket, is a member of the mustard family and grows wild in the Mediterranean region. Its peppery flavor is a favorite in southern Italy and France. It is available in specialty markets and some groceries.

RICE AND SPINACH SALAD WITH ORIENTAL VINAIGRETTE

SALAD

1 tablespoon safflower oil
½ cup pine nuts or slivered almonds
1½ cups cooked rice, preferably brown
½ pound fresh spinach leaves (about 4 cups), cut into julienne strips
2 scallions, chopped
1 11-ounce can mandarin orange segments, drained, or ½ cup halved grapes
1 8-ounce can sliced water chestnuts, drained

ORIENTAL VINAIGRETTE

3 tablespoons safflower oil
2 tablespoons rice vinegar
2 tablespoons soy sauce
½ teaspoon black pepper
1 clove garlic, minced
¼ teaspoon ginger powder

Garnish: *blanched peapods, halved red or green grapes, currants, or raisins, optional*

In a small skillet, heat oil. Sauté pine nuts until lightly browned. Set aside to cool.

In a large bowl, toss together rice, spinach, scallions, mandarin oranges, and water chestnuts.

In a small bowl, whisk together dressing ingredients; pour over salad. Add pine nuts and toss. Garnish with peapods, grapes, currants, or raisins.

4 to 6 servings

VARIATIONS

◆ substitute arugula for spinach
◆ omit mandarin oranges. Garnish salad with orange sec-

tions from 1 orange quickly sautéed in 1 tablespoon margarine with 1 tablespoon sugar added; chill, cut into 1-inch pieces; toss into salad.
♦ for a hotter flavor, add a few drops of hot pepper sauce or a dash of dried red pepper flakes to the dressing
♦ substitute Chutney Dressing (p. 60) for the Oriental Vinaigrette

With the combination of beans and tofu forming a complete protein, this is an ideal main-course salad for warm days. Serve with crusty bread. Small portions served on a bed of lettuce also make a nice first course.

ADVANCE PREPARATION
Salad may be served immediately or will keep for several days in the refrigerator.

HINTS
♦ Beans should be served with seeds, nuts, grains, dairy products, or eggs to form a complete protein.
♦ Parsley will chop very finely if it is thoroughly dried with a dish towel before it is chopped. Otherwise the pieces will tend to stick together and will not separate into fine flakes.

TERIYAKI SALAD

SALAD
1 15-ounce can chick peas, drained and rinsed (1³/₄ cups)
1¹/₂ cups sliced mushrooms (4 ounces)
1 tomato, cubed
1 scallion, chopped
¹/₂ green bell pepper, coarsely chopped
¹/₂ pound firm tofu, cut into ¹/₂-inch cubes
¹/₄ cup chopped fresh parsley

DRESSING
2 tablespoons rice vinegar
2 tablespoons safflower oil
1 tablespoon Dijon mustard
1 teaspoon soy sauce
1 clove garlic, finely minced
¹/₄ teaspoon ginger powder
¹/₄ teaspoon coarsely ground black pepper
2 tablespoons sesame seeds, toasted or untoasted

lettuce leaves

Garnish: *sweet red pepper strips, optional*

In a salad bowl, toss together salad ingredients.
   In a small mixing bowl, combine dressing ingredients. Pour over salad and toss. Using a slotted spoon, arrange mixture on lettuce leaves. Garnish with pepper strips.
   4 servings

Couscous is an ideal grain for the 15-minute cook because it is so quick to prepare. For variety, add chick peas, raw sunflower seeds, and other vegetables such as shredded carrots, or sweet red pepper strips.

ADVANCE PREPARATION

This salad will keep well for several days in a covered container in the refrigerator. However, I prefer to add the dressing just before serving because it is absorbed as the salad sets.

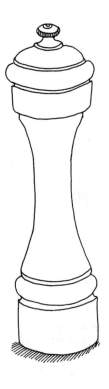

COUSCOUS-CURRANT SALAD WITH LEMON DRESSING

SALAD
1 cup couscous
1 cup vegetable stock or water
1 teaspoon olive oil
¼ cup pine nuts, slivered almonds, or raw cashews
1 stalk celery, diced
1 scallion, chopped
2 tablespoons chopped fresh parsley
⅓ cup currants or raisins

LEMON DRESSING
¼ cup fresh lemon juice
2 tablespoons olive oil
¼ teaspoon cinnamon
¼ teaspoon black pepper
¼ teaspoon turmeric
few drops of hot pepper sauce

Garnish: *asparagus tips or finely chopped fresh chives, optional*

In a large bowl, stir together dry couscous and stock or water. Let stand, covered, until liquid is completely absorbed, 5 to 10 minutes. Toss lightly with a fork.

Meanwhile, in a small skillet, heat olive oil. Add nuts and sauté until golden brown.

Prepare remaining salad ingredients. In a small bowl, combine dressing ingredients.

When couscous has softened, toss in nuts, celery, scallion,

parsley, and currants or raisins. Add dressing and toss again. Garnish with asparagus tips or chives. Serve immediately or allow to cool.

4 servings

VARIATIONS

◆ substitute cooked rice for couscous
◆ substitute ¼ cup Chutney Dressing (p. 60) for Lemon Dressing
◆ in the dressing, substitute 1 to 2 teaspoons curry powder for the cinnamon and turmeric

The goodness of pasta, crisp-tender vegetables, and cheese combine artfully to produce a beautiful salad. This is my personal favorite; I have served it in a buffet for fifty and at small family gatherings.

ADVANCE PREPARATION

This salad is ideal for advance preparation. Remove from refrigerator about 30 minutes before serving. I usually add the dressing no more than 2 hours in advance because it tends to be absorbed into the pasta.

HINTS

◆ The ridges in corkscrew pasta help the dressing to adhere to the noodles.
◆ The tender leaves of watercress have a peppery flavor.

PASTA SALAD PRIMAVERA

8 ounces corkscrew pasta (fusilli or rotini)
2 cups broccoli florets
1 cup peas
1 small zucchini, cubed
1 sweet red pepper, seeded and diced
1 Italian plum tomato, diced
2 scallions, chopped
4 ounces mozzarella cheese, cut into cubes (1 cup)
1 cup Herbed Tomato Sauce (p. 75), Yogurt-Parmesan Dressing (p. 76), or Creamy Italian Dressing (p. 76)
freshly grated Parmesan cheese
freshly ground black pepper

Garnish: *fresh parsley sprigs, fresh watercress leaves, or fresh basil leaves and sautéed pine nuts, optional*

Boil a large pot of water; cook pasta until *al dente*.

While pasta is cooking, steam broccoli, peas, and zucchini. When crisp-tender, remove from steamer and place in a colander under cold running water to cool. Drain well.

When pasta is cooked *al dente*, drain, rinse under cold water, then drain well again.

In a large bowl, toss together pasta, broccoli, peas, zuc-

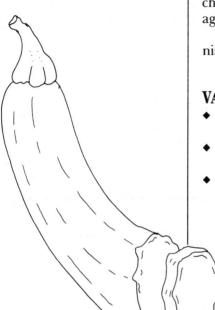

chini, red pepper, tomato, scallions, and mozzarella. Toss again with dressing.

Top each serving with Parmesan and pepper. Add garnish.

4 generous servings

VARIATIONS

- ♦ substitute or add other steamed vegetables such as peapods, carrots, mushrooms, cauliflower, or asparagus
- ♦ for additional protein, add cubed tofu, chopped walnuts, or legumes such as chick peas
- ♦ for the suggested dressings, substitute ½ cup Honey-Poppyseed Dressing (p. 57), Tangy Honey-Mustard Dressing (p. 58), Vinaigrette Dressing (p. 59), or Light Pesto Vinaigrette (p. 68). (These are thinner dressings so less is required to moisten the salad.)

Pasta salads travel well. This is one of my summer picnic favorites!

ADVANCE PREPARATION

This salad is ideal for advance preparation. Remove from refrigerator about 30 minutes before serving. I usually add the dressing no more than 2 hours in advance because it tends to be absorbed into the pasta.

PASTA-ASPARAGUS SALAD

8 ounces corkscrew pasta (fusilli or rotini)
¾ pound fresh asparagus, trimmed and cut into 3-inch lengths
½ pint cherry tomatoes, halved
2 carrots, shredded
1 sweet red pepper, coarsely chopped
1 cup Herbed Tomato Sauce (p. 75), or Yogurt-Parmesan Dressing (p. 76), or Creamy Italian Dressing (p. 76)

Garnish: *fresh basil leaves or fresh parsley sprigs, optional*

Boil a large pot of water; cook pasta until *al dente*.

While pasta is cooking, steam asparagus until crisp-

HINTS

◆ When buying asparagus, choose spears with firm green stalks and hard-closed tips. Avoid asparagus that is limp and yellowed. For cooking, select stalks with similar diameters.

◆ Asparagus, like pasta, should be cooked until *al dente.*

tender. Remove from steamer, place in a colander, and run under cold water to cool; drain well.

When pasta is done, drain, rinse under cold water, then drain well.

In a large bowl, toss together pasta and vegetables. Toss again with dressing. Garnish with basil leaves or parsley sprigs.

4 servings

VARIATIONS

◆ substitute pimiento for red pepper

◆ for the pasta dressings, substitute ½ cup Honey-Poppy-seed Dressing (p. 57), Tangy Honey-Mustard Dressing (p. 58), Vinaigrette Dressing (p. 59), or Light Pesto Vinaigrette (p. 68). (These are thinner dressings so less is required to moisten the salad.)

This sauce is my personal favorite on the Pasta Salad Primavera.

ADVANCE PREPARATION

May be prepared up to 3 days in advance and refrigerated. Stir before tossing with pasta.

HINTS

◆ Refrigerate opened containers of olive oil. The oil will cloud and solidify, but it will clear and liquefy when set at room temperature for a few minutes.

◆ Store dried herbs out of direct sunlight and in jars or tins rather than in cardboard boxes.

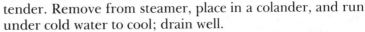

HERBED TOMATO SAUCE

1 8-ounce can unsalted tomato sauce (1 cup)
2 tablespoons safflower oil, olive oil, or a combination
1 tablespoon red wine vinegar
1 clove garlic, very finely minced
1 teaspoon basil
1 teaspoon oregano
1 teaspoon black pepper

Stir ingredients together and fold into pasta and vegetables.
makes 1 cup

VARIATIONS

◆ this sauce is also delicious served warm on warm pasta, vegetables, or over a cheese omelet

◆ omit oil to reduce calories

This is my favorite for the Pasta-Asparagus Salad. It requires no cooking and is a snap to prepare while the pasta is cooking.

ADVANCE PREPARATION

May be prepared early the day it is to be served and refrigerated. Stir before tossing with pasta.

A variation on the classic, this flavorful dressing is low in fat yet high in calcium and protein.

ADVANCE PREPARATION

This dressing may be prepared early the day it is to be served; refrigerate. Stir before tossing with pasta.

YOGURT-PARMESAN DRESSING

1 cup plain yogurt
¼ cup grated Parmesan cheese
1 clove garlic, finely minced
1 tablespoon lemon juice
1 teaspoon dill weed
1 teaspoon black pepper

Stir ingredients together and fold into pasta and vegetables.
  makes 1 cup

CREAMY ITALIAN DRESSING

⅓ cup low-fat cottage cheese
⅓ cup yogurt
2 tablespoons safflower oil or olive oil
2 tablespoons finely chopped onion
1 clove garlic, finely minced
1 tablespoon lemon juice
1 tablespoon Dijon mustard
1 teaspoon basil
1 teaspoon oregano
1 teaspoon minced fresh parsley
½ teaspoon pepper

Place cottage cheese, yogurt, safflower oil, onion, garlic, lemon juice, and mustard in a food processor; process until smooth. Stir in remaining ingredients.
  Fold into pasta salad.
  makes 1 cup

VARIATION

◆ substitute ricotta cheese for the cottage cheese adding 2 tablespoons milk and 2 tablespoons Parmesan cheese

If you are tired of the same old vegetables in your pasta salad, try this salad with an Oriental flair. Though not authentic, it is delicious!

ADVANCE PREPARATION

This salad is ideal for advance preparation. Remove from refrigerator about 30 minutes before serving. I usually add the dressing no more than 2 hours in advance because it tends to be absorbed into the pasta.

HINTS

◆ When cooking pasta for a spicy salad such as this, adding 1 teaspoon hot pepper sauce to the cooking water will infuse the pasta with a subtle pepper flavor, a simple way to add flavor without salt.

◆ To string peapods, pull downward from the stem.

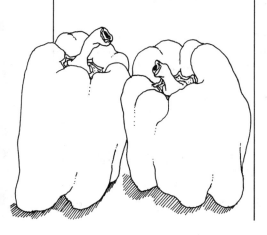

SZECHWAN PASTA SALAD WITH HOT PEPPER VINAIGRETTE

SALAD

8 ounces bow tie pasta
3 cups broccoli florets
1/4 pound fresh peapods, strings removed
1 sweet red pepper, cut into thin strips
3 scallions, cut into 1/2-inch pieces

HOT PEPPER VINAIGRETTE

1/3 cup safflower oil
1/3 cup red wine vinegar
2 tablespoons honey
1 clove garlic, finely minced
2 tablespoons sesame seeds, toasted or untoasted
2 teaspoons hot pepper sauce
1/2 teaspoon ginger powder
pinch of cayenne pepper

Garnish: *fresh watercress leaves and sautéed pine nuts, optional*

Boil a large pot of water; cook pasta until *al dente*.

While pasta is cooking, blanch broccoli and peapods. Combine dressing ingredients. When pasta is done, drain and rinse under cold water. Drain well.

Place pasta in a bowl and toss with broccoli, peapods, red pepper, and scallions. Pour on dressing; toss to coat evenly. Garnish with watercress leaves and sautéed pine nuts.

4 servings

VARIATIONS

◆ steam vegetables instead of blanching
◆ add or substitute other vegetables such as mushrooms or steamed asparagus

This is a recipe that my neighbor and good friend from Thailand shared with me. It is authentic, spicy, and one of my favorites.

ADVANCE PREPARATION

This salad can be made early the day it is to be served.

HINT

◆ Cellophane noodles are also called bean thread, mung bean sticks, sai-fun noodles, or pea starch noodles. Made from mung bean flour and water, they are available in Oriental food stores and in the gourmet section of many supermarkets.

THAI NOODLE SALAD

8 to 10 ounces cellophane noodles
1 cup unsalted peanuts
4 tablespoons minced gingerroot or 1-inch-thick piece ginger about 4 inches long
1 hot red chili pepper, seeds removed
1/4 cup chopped fresh basil, mint, or coriander
1/2 cup lime juice, lemon juice, or white vinegar
1/4 cup soy sauce
1/4 cup sugar

Garnishes: *sweet red pepper or green bell pepper rings and unsalted peanuts, optional*

Bring a pot of water to a boil. Meanwhile, in a large bowl, soak cellophane noodles in hot tap water for about 5 minutes. Drain noodles, then soak in boiling water for an additional 5 minutes, or until they are softened and clear. Drain well and, using kitchen shears, cut into shorter lengths. Set noodles aside to cool.

In a food processor or electric mincer, combine peanuts, ginger, and hot pepper. Process until well mixed. In a large bowl, toss mixture with noodles. Toss again with basil, mint, or coriander.

In a measuring cup, combine remaining ingredients; stir until sugar is dissolved. Pour over salad and toss until dressing is evenly distributed. Garnish with pepper rings and unsalted peanuts.

4 to 6 servings

VARIATIONS

◆ add 2 cloves garlic, minced
◆ for a milder flavor, substitute green chili pepper or jalapeño pepper for hot red chili pepper, or use less hot red chili pepper
◆ substitute 1/2 teaspoon dried crushed red pepper for the fresh chili pepper

This colorful salad combines grains and pasta with crunchy vegetables; it contains protein and makes an interesting main-course meal. This is one of my favorites.

ADVANCE PREPARATION

Toss together salad ingredients and prepare dressing in advance. Combine just before serving. If allowed to set, some of the dressing will be absorbed into the pasta and grain.

HINT

◆ In this salad, the couscous, pasta, peanuts, and peanut butter combine to form a high-quality complete protein.

PASTA AND COUSCOUS SALAD WITH SPICY PEANUT DRESSING

SALAD

6 ounces spinach ribbon noodles (3 1/2 cups uncooked)
1/2 cup couscous
1/2 cup hot vegetable stock or water
1 sweet red pepper, cut into strips 1/4 × 1 1/2 inches
1/2 cup roasted unsalted peanuts
2 scallions, thinly sliced
1/4 cup chopped fresh parsley

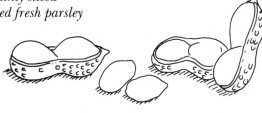

SPICY PEANUT DRESSING

1/4 cup rice vinegar
3 tablespoons olive oil
3 tablespoons smooth peanut butter
1 clove garlic, finely minced
1 tablespoon honey
1/4 teaspoon cayenne pepper

Garnish: *orange slices, mandarin orange segments, or pineapple slices and raisins, optional*

Boil a large pot of water; cook pasta until *al dente*.

While pasta is cooking, in a small bowl, stir together dry couscous and stock or water. Let stand, covered, until liquid is completely absorbed, 5 to 10 minutes. Toss lightly with a fork.

Meanwhile, in a large bowl, toss together remaining salad ingredients.

In a small bowl, whisk together dressing ingredients.

When pasta is done, drain well and rinse under cold

water. Drain well again. Add with couscous to salad ingredients. Pour on dressing; toss again. Top with garnish.

4 to 6 servings

VARIATIONS

◆ substitute other varieties of pasta for spinach noodles
◆ substitute cooked millet for couscous (see p. 15 for cooking instructions)
◆ substitute cooked chick peas for the peanuts

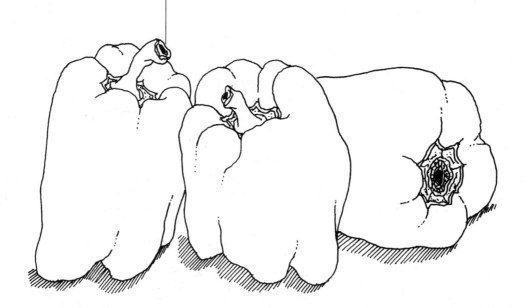

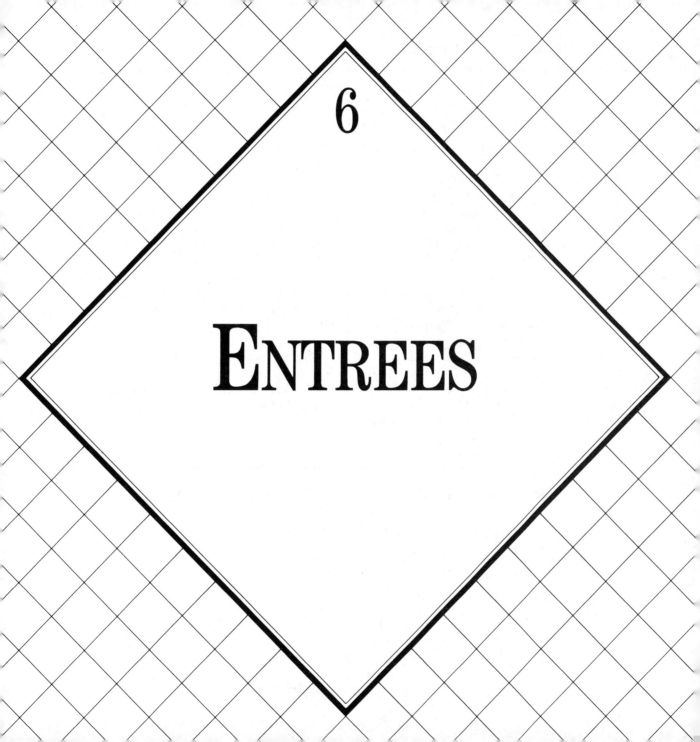

6

ENTREES

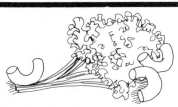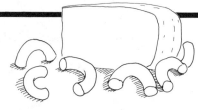

I f you have only 15 minutes, most of the recipes in this chapter will stand on their own, with the addition of a simple salad. Each dish includes a protein source, and a wide variety of vegetables, legumes, nuts, cheeses, and seasonings have been used.

Many pasta and rice dishes are included because of their increasing popularity. They are also the perfect bases for many meatless sauces and toppers because of their neutral flavor. They are substantial, too, since they are complex carbohydrates, the most efficient source of fuel for the body. Combined with a protein source (in the sauce or topper), they provide a satisfying and nutritionally complete meal.

I have relied less on egg dishes for the main course because I believe eggs should be served sparingly. At our house we usually enjoy only one main-dish egg meal per week; included are recipes for some of my favorites.

I have stated earlier my attraction to ethnic recipes because of their use of natural ingredients and interesting flavors. In this chapter I have adapted some of my favorites.

These recipes are simple enough to make for your family on a daily basis yet are "gourmet" enough to please your discriminating guests.

With a little advance planning, this can be the main course for a special picnic. Accompany it with French bread and Pesto Herb Spread (p. 23), and Maple Oranges Amandine (p. 130) for dessert.

PASTA SHELLS WITH LEMON VINAIGRETTE

12 jumbo pasta shells

FILLING
1½ cups ricotta cheese, part skim variety
3 tablespoons chopped fresh chives or 1 tablespoon dried chives or
   1 chopped scallion
2 tablespoons grated lemon peel
¾ teaspoon black pepper
½ cup very finely chopped almonds

ADVANCE PREPARATION

This dish may be assembled early on the day it is to be served; refrigerate. Serve chilled or allow to come to room temperature.

HINT

◆ Olive oil is a mono-saturated fat; it does not have an effect on blood cholesterol levels.

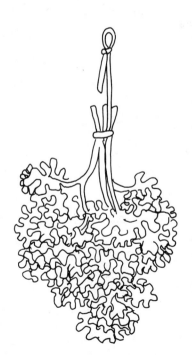

LEMON VINAIGRETTE

¼ cup lemon juice
2 tablespoons olive oil
1 teaspoon Dijon mustard
2 tablespoons chopped fresh parsley
1 tablespoon basil
1 clove garlic, very finely minced

Garnish: *sliced almonds, cherry tomatoes, lemon wedges, fresh basil leaves or fresh parsley sprigs, or sautéed pine nuts, and Parmesan cheese, optional*

Bring a large pot of water to a boil; cook pasta until *al dente.*

While pasta is cooking, in a medium-size bowl, combine filling ingredients. Set aside.

In a large bowl, combine dressing ingredients. Set aside.

When pasta is done, drain well, rinse under cold water, and drain well again. Toss shells with dressing to coat.

Stuff shells with filling mixture, allowing 1 heaping tablespoon for each. Arrange on a serving platter. Drizzle each with some of the remaining dressing. Top with garnishes and serve immediately or chill.

4 servings

VARIATIONS

◆ substitute 6 pieces of lasagna for pasta shells, spread each with filling, then roll up jelly-roll fashion
◆ substitute ½ to 1 cup mashed tofu for part of ricotta cheese, or for all of the ricotta if you are a real tofu fan
◆ in place of the Lemon Vinaigrette, prepare the Herbed Tomato Sauce (p. 75); follow the same procedure of tossing the shells with the dressing. Pour half of the remaining dressing on the serving platter, arrange shells, and top with remaining sauce.

The aroma of fresh basil! If fresh basil is unavailable, dried basil is out of the question. Instead, try Spinach-Parsley Pesto (p. 23).

ADVANCE PREPARATION

Pesto may be made in advance according to instructions on page 22. Toss pesto with pasta just before serving.

HINTS

◆ Basil is easy to grow at home in a garden or window box. Hearty plants may even last in the winter indoors if placed in a sunny spot. For minimal effort, the bonus of having fresh basil on hand is its own reward.

◆ Freshly grated Parmesan cheese has a flavor far superior to the pre-servatives-laden type available in jars.

PASTA AL PESTO

8 ounces pasta (preferably linguine)
1 recipe Pesto (p. 22)
3 carrots, thinly sliced
2 tablespoons safflower oil or olive oil
3 small zucchini, thinly sliced
¼ pound peapods

Garnish: *freshly ground black pepper and grated Parmesan cheese, optional*

Boil a large pot of water; cook pasta until *al dente*.

While pasta is cooking, prepare pesto; set aside, covered.

Steam carrots. Meanwhile, in a skillet, heat oil. Add zucchini and peapods. Stir continuously until crisp-tender.

When pasta is done, drain well; toss pesto with noodles until they are coated. Then toss in vegetables. Garnish with pepper and cheese.

6 servings

VARIATIONS

◆ add ½ cup Parmesan cheese to Pesto
◆ add or substitute other steamed or sautéed vegetables such as mushrooms, peas, or sweet red pepper

Although it is so simple, this is an elegant and tasty pasta sauce. I like to serve it with a spinach and mushroom salad.

ADVANCE PREPARATION

Sauce may be made in advance and refrigerated. Bring to room temperature before tossing with hot pasta as you are ready to serve.

HINTS

◆ Pine nuts are also referred to as "pignolia."
◆ Freshly ground black pepper has a taste far superior to ready ground.
◆ Ricotta is made from the whey that remains after the production of such cheeses as provolone and mozzarella. The whey is blended with whole or skim milk and *voilà*, ricotta! Ricotta is therefore not a true cheese because it is not made from curd.

PASTA WITH HERBED RICOTTA AND PINE NUTS

8 ounces pasta (preferably spinach noodles)
2 tablespoons softened margarine
½ cup pine nuts
1 small onion, chopped (about ¼ cup)
¾ cup ricotta cheese, preferably part skim variety
2 tablespoons chopped fresh parsley
1 tablespoon tarragon
1 tablespoon lemon juice
½ teaspoon grated lemon rind
½ teaspoon pepper
freshly ground pepper

Garnish: *halved cherry tomatoes, fresh parsley sprigs, sweet red pepper strips, steamed asparagus spears, or sautéed mushroom caps dusted with paprika, optional*

Boil a large pot of water; cook pasta until *al dente*.
　While pasta is cooking, in a small skillet, melt margarine. Add pine nuts and onion, stirring occasionally over medium heat for about 5 minutes, until pine nuts are lightly browned and onion is softened. Set aside.
　In a small bowl, beat cheese with remaining ingredients. Stir in pine nuts and onion.
　When pasta is done, drain well; toss with sauce. Top with freshly ground pepper and garnishes.
　4 servings

VARIATIONS

◆ substitute raw cashews for pine nuts
◆ substitute basil for tarragon
◆ add ½ cup chopped, cooked spinach to ricotta-sauce mixture

Typical of the new lighter Italian cuisine, this sauce tossed with pasta is delicious served either hot or cold.

ADVANCE PREPARATION
Sauce may be made in advance and refrigerated. Bring to room temperature before tossing with hot pasta as you are ready to serve.

HINTS
◆ Walnuts and dairy products combine to form a complete protein. Nuts and seeds add important variety to a meatless diet.
◆ For your information: All recipes in this book calling for margarine have been tested using the unsalted variety with favorable results; consider using it if sodium intake is a concern to you.

PASTA WITH RICOTTA-WALNUT SAUCE

8 ounces pasta (preferably vermicelli)

RICOTTA-WALNUT SAUCE
½ cup ricotta cheese
½ cup plain yogurt
1 tablespoon margarine, softened
2 cloves garlic, minced
½ cup chopped walnuts (about 2 ounces)
¼ cup grated Parmesan cheese (about 1 ounce)
½ cup chopped fresh parsley
1 tablespoon chopped fresh basil or 1 teaspoon dried basil
½ teaspoon black pepper

Garnish: *cherry tomatoes or broccoli florets, more grated Parmesan cheese, and sprinkling of freshly ground black pepper, optional*

Boil a large pot of water; cook pasta until *al dente*.

While pasta is cooking, in bowl of a food processor, place ricotta, yogurt, margarine, garlic, walnuts, and cheese; process until smooth. Stir in remaining ingredients.

When pasta is done, drain well. Toss with sauce. Top with garnishes and serve immediately.

4 servings

VARIATIONS
◆ when sauce is tossed with pasta, add steamed vegetables such as peas, broccoli, cut green beans, and spinach; peas are especially good
◆ serve cold as a pasta salad
◆ for Fettucine Almost Alfredo, substitute ¼ cup milk and ¼ cup vegetable stock for the yogurt; omit garlic, walnuts, parsley, and basil; garnish with almond slices, parsley sprigs, and cherry tomatoes or cut steamed asparagus

A treat for curry lovers. The chick peas and pasta complement each other to form a complete protein.

ADVANCE PREPARATION

Sauce may be made in advance, refrigerated, and reheated before serving.

HINTS

◆ Vegans are strict vegetarians who eat neither animal flesh nor animal products, including all dairy products. This dish would fit into a vegan diet.

◆ To make scallion curls, slice the green part *very* thin lengthwise. Drop into ice water. Curls will form in about 15 minutes.

CHICK PEA–ZUCCHINI CURRY

8 ounces pasta (preferably thin egg noodles or whole wheat spaghetti)
2 tablespoons safflower oil
1 small onion, chopped (¼ cup)
1 clove garlic, minced
1½ cups sliced mushrooms (4 ounces)
2 medium-size zucchini, sliced
1 large tomato, cubed
1 15-ounce can chick peas, drained and rinsed (1½ cups)
1 6-ounce can tomato paste, preferably unsalted (⅔ cup)
1 cup water
2 teaspoons curry powder, or more to taste
¼ teaspoon black pepper

Garnish: *scallion curls, optional*

Boil a large pot of water; cook pasta until *al dente*.

While pasta is cooking, in a saucepan, heat oil. Add onion, garlic, mushrooms, and zucchini. Sauté until zucchini is tender but not mushy. Stir in remaining ingredients and cook over medium heat, covered, for about 8 minutes.

When pasta is done, drain well.

Spoon vegetables over pasta. Garnish with scallion curls. *4 servings*

VARIATIONS

◆ add 1 to 2 teaspoons finely minced gingerroot; sauté with vegetables
◆ serve on beds of hot cooked brown rice
◆ serve on couscous

This combination of flavors is wonderful—the delicately flavored sauce is one of my favorites.

ADVANCE PREPARATION

Chinese Tahini Sauce may be prepared up to 2 days in advance and refrigerated. Bring to room temperature and toss with hot pasta just before serving. (Even if you plan to serve this dish cold or at room temperature, toss the dressing with hot pasta; then cool.)

HINTS

◆ Tahini, made of ground sesame seeds, is also called sesame butter. It can be purchased in jars in natural food stores and in some supermarkets. Refrigerate it after opening and stir the oils back in before using. Darker varieties made from toasted seeds are more intense in flavor, so use sparingly.

◆ Chili paste with garlic is sometimes labeled Chili Sauce or Chinese Chili Sauce. Garlic and hot pepper sauce can be substituted.

◆ Chinese wheat noodles are made of wheat flour, cornstarch, salt, and sugar. The noodles are compacted into cubes. To cook, break the cubes and drop into boiling water. When water returns to a boil, cook for 3 minutes and drain. They may be served as is or patted dry and sautéed in oil until lightly browned.

PASTA WITH CHINESE TAHINI SAUCE

8 ounces pasta (preferably buckwheat noodles or Chinese wheat noodles)
1 cup peas

CHINESE TAHINI SAUCE

2 tablespoons tahini
1 tablespoon rice vinegar
1 tablespoon soy sauce
1 tablespoon sesame oil, preferably toasted sesame oil
2 teaspoons chili paste with garlic
1 teaspoon minced gingerroot
2 tablespoons vegetable stock or water
dash of freshly ground black pepper

Garnish: *scallion curls, fresh coriander sprigs, toasted sesame seeds, or chopped dry-roasted unsalted peanuts, optional*

Bring a large pot of water to a boil; cook pasta until *al dente*.

While pasta is cooking, steam peas. In a large bowl, combine remaining ingredients.

When pasta is done, drain well. Toss dressing with pasta; add peas and toss again. Top with garnish.

4 servings

VARIATIONS

◆ sauté 6 ounces fresh chopped spinach in 1 tablespoon safflower oil until limp; toss with noodles and sauce

◆ add or substitute other vegetables such as sautéed sliced mushrooms, steamed broccoli, steamed sliced carrots, blanched peapods, sweet red peppers, or scallions; if you add several, the amount of dressing may need to be increased

◆ chill or bring to room temperature and serve as a side dish or salad

Peanut butter lovers, beware! This sauce can be addictive! Serve this recipe either hot or chilled. The sauce is equally delicious on cold vegetable salads as on hot linguine. If you like your food spicy, adding more dry crushed red pepper can make this dish fiery!

ADVANCE PREPARATION

Szechwan Peanut Dressing may be made up to 2 days in advance and refrigerated. Bring to room temperature and toss with hot pasta just before serving. (Even if you plan to serve this dish cold or at room temperature, toss the dressing with hot pasta; then cool.)

PASTA WITH SZECHWAN PEANUT DRESSING

8 ounces pasta (preferably linguine)
2 cups broccoli florets

SZECHWAN PEANUT DRESSING   *makes ³/₄ cup*
¹/₃ cup peanut butter, smooth or chunky
¹/₂ cup hot vegetable stock or hot water
1 teaspoon soy sauce
2 tablespoons rice vinegar
2 tablespoons safflower oil
2 cloves garlic, minced
¹/₂ teaspoon dry crushed red pepper (1 teaspoon if you prefer spicy flavoring)

2 cups cherry tomatoes

Garnish: *chopped scallions, optional*

Bring a large pot of water to a boil; cook pasta until *al dente*.
     While pasta is cooking, steam broccoli florets.
     In a medium-size mixing bowl, whisk together peanut butter and stock or water until smooth. Stir in remaining dressing ingredients.
     When pasta is done, drain well. Pour sauce over pasta; toss to coat well. Add broccoli and tomatoes; toss again. Garnish with chopped scallions.
     4 to 6 servings

VARIATIONS
◆ try Szechwan Peanut Dressing as a warm topping on steamed vegetables, especially on green beans, broccoli, or cauliflower
◆ make extra dressing to refrigerate and serve later on chilled steamed green beans or broccoli or on Indonesian Vegetable Salad (p. 64)

Here is another way to use a basic marinara sauce.

ADVANCE PREPARATION

Marinara Sauce may be made up to 3 days in advance and reheated; prepare spinach and pasta and assemble just before serving.

HINTS

◆ For added protein as well as tastiness, after pasta has been cooked and drained, melt 1 tablespoon margarine in the pasta pot, return pasta to pot, and toss to coat. Lightly beat 2 eggs (or 3 whites); pour over pasta, tossing over medium heat until egg is cooked. Add a dash of pepper. I occasionally serve this as a speedy main course with a steamed vegetable.

◆ Compared to most cooked vegetables, spinach freezes and thaws well.

PASTA MARINARA ON BEDS OF SPINACH

1 recipe Marinara Sauce (p. 24)
1 10-ounce package frozen chopped spinach
8 ounces pasta (preferably spaghetti)
dash of freshly ground black pepper
juice of ½ lemon

Garnish: *grated Parmesan cheese, freshly ground black pepper, and sautéed pine nuts, optional*

Prepare Marinara Sauce.

While Marinara Sauce is simmering, cook spinach; drain well. Also cook pasta until *al dente;* drain well.

To serve, place a bed of spinach on each of 4 dinner plates. Sprinkle with pepper and drizzle with lemon juice. Add a layer of pasta. Top with Marinara Sauce and garnishes.

4 servings

VARIATIONS

◆ stir other steamed vegetables into sauce
◆ substitute hot cooked brown rice for pasta

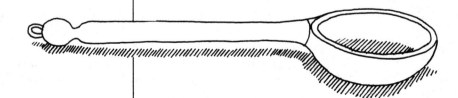

I cannot make this dish without thinking of the day my slim husband ate the entire recipe. Apparently this is his favorite pasta dish!

ADVANCE PREPARATION

This dish is at its best when prepared and served immediately, but leftovers can be reheated.

HINTS

◆ Ricotta cheese can be purchased in most dairy departments in a "part skim" variety that reduces the calorie content by less than half but does not noticeably alter the flavor.

◆ Lacto-ovo vegetarians eat no animal flesh but do eat animal products such as milk, cheese, and eggs.

TRIPLE CHEESE–POPPYSEED NOODLES

8 ounces wide egg noodles
½ cup ricotta cheese, preferably part skim variety
½ cup plain yogurt
½ cup cottage cheese (unsalted works well)
1 2-ounce jar chopped pimiento
1 clove garlic, finely minced
1 tablespoon poppyseed
½ teaspoon hot pepper sauce
½ teaspoon black pepper
½ cup grated Cheddar cheese (2 ounces)
dash of paprika

Garnish: *fresh parsley sprigs, steamed broccoli florets, or steamed asparagus spears, optional*

Boil a large pot of water; cook noodles until *al dente.*

While noodles are cooking, in a medium-size mixing bowl, combine remaining ingredients except Cheddar cheese and paprika.

When noodles are done, drain well. Return them to pot. Pour in sauce mixture and toss to coat.

Pour mixture into a microwave-proof casserole dish. Sprinkle with grated Cheddar cheese; top with paprika. Heat in microwave, high setting, for 3 minutes, to melt cheese and heat through. Top with garnish.

4 to 6 servings

VARIATIONS

◆ stir in steamed vegetables
◆ serve over a bed of steamed spinach
◆ bake in oven at 375° F. for about 25 minutes. Though it takes longer, the crispy edges are delicious!

Simple, quick, and more interesting than the kind we ate as kids.

ADVANCE PREPARATION

Best made just before serving.

HINT

◆ The best margarines are made with polyunsaturated safflower or corn oil. Other margarines contain less expensive vegetable oils such as coconut oil and cottonseed oil. Read labels! If you see the word "hydrogenated" in the ingredients list, the product contains saturated fat.

MACARONI AND CHEESE WITH VEGETABLES

8 ounces pasta (preferably bow ties or large ribbed macaroni)
3 tablespoons margarine, divided
1 tablespoon unbleached flour
½ cup vegetable stock
¾ cup milk
½ cup grated Cheddar cheese (2 ounces)
½ cup grated Parmesan cheese (2 ounces)
1 tablespoon chopped fresh parsley
1 teaspoon basil
¼ teaspoon paprika
¼ teaspoon black pepper
2 cups broccoli florets
1 medium-size sweet red pepper, coarsely chopped
1 cup sliced mushrooms (3 ounces)
2 scallions, sliced

Garnish: scallion curls, optional

Bring a large pot of water to a boil; cook pasta until *al dente.*

While pasta is cooking, in a medium-size saucepan, melt 2 tablespoons of the margarine. Remove from heat; add flour and stir until blended in. Whisk in stock and milk, stirring over medium heat until mixture comes to a boil and thickens. Reduce heat to low. Stir in cheeses and seasonings. Continue stirring until cheese is melted. Remove from heat and set aside.

In a large skillet, melt remaining 1 tablespoon margarine. Add remaining ingredients. Cook vegetables, stirring constantly, for about 5 minutes, until crisp-tender; reduce heat to low. When noodles are done, drain well. Toss with vegetables; stir in cheese sauce. Garnish with scallion curls.

6 servings

This is undoubtedly one of the quickest main courses, but no one needs to know your secret. It is delicious!

ADVANCE PREPARATION
This dish must be prepared just before serving.

HINT
◆ For a special touch, serve pasta on heated plates.

HERBED MACARONI PARMESAN

8 ounces macaroni noodles
3 tablespoons margarine
¹/₂ cup grated Parmesan cheese (2 ounces)
1 Italian plum tomato, chopped (at room temperature)
2 tablespoons minced fresh basil or 2 teaspoons dried basil
2 tablespoons chopped fresh parsley
dash of freshly ground black pepper

Garnish: *broccoli florets, optional*

Bring a large pot of water to a boil; cook pasta until *al dente*.
When pasta is done, drain well. Toss hot noodles with margarine to melt. Add other ingredients. Toss to combine. Garnish with broccoli florets.
4 servings

VARIATION
◆ add sautéed mushroom slices or your choice of steamed chopped vegetables

Colorful and loaded with Chinese flavor, this dish is a meal in itself with rice. For variety, serve it over couscous or pasta such as buckwheat noodles.

ADVANCE PREPARATION

Vegetables may be sliced in advance, but further preparations are not recommended until just before serving.

SWEET AND SOUR TOFU

3 to 4 cups hot cooked brown rice

SWEET AND SOUR SAUCE   *makes 1³/₄ cups*
1 cup pineapple juice
¹/₃ cup rice vinegar
2 tablespoons soy sauce
2 tablespoons cornstarch
3 tablespoons tomato paste
2 tablespoons honey
1 tablespoon minced gingerroot
dash of white pepper

2 tablespoons safflower oil
2 medium-size carrots, thinly sliced
1 medium-size sweet red pepper, sliced
1 medium-size green bell pepper, sliced
1 medium-size onion, sliced
1 clove garlic, minced
³/₄ pound firm tofu, cut into ¹/₂-inch cubes
1 large tomato, cut into wedges
1 8-ounce can pineapple chunks or tidbits in own juice, drained (1 cup)
2 tablespoons toasted sesame seeds

HINTS

◆ Tofu is low in calories, rich in calcium and iron, and cholesterol-free. Be certain to check the freshness dates on tofu packages. Fresh tofu is always the best. When you bring tofu home from the store, rinse and drain it, refrigerate in fresh water. If the water is changed daily, the tofu will remain fresh for 7 to 10 days.

◆ Tomato paste is available in tubes at many groceries and specialty stores. It is ideal for recipes calling for less than a 6-ounce can.

Garnish: *scallion curls, chopped raw cashews, chopped peanuts, or sprig of fresh coriander, optional*

Cook or reheat rice (see p. 14).

In a small bowl, whisk together pineapple juice, vinegar, and soy sauce. Add cornstarch, stirring until smooth. Stir in remaining sauce ingredients. Set aside.

In a large skillet or wok, heat safflower oil on high. Sauté carrots, peppers, onion, and garlic until carrot is crisp-tender, about 5 minutes.

Stir sauce, pour over vegetables, stirring until sauce thickens. Gently fold in remaining ingredients.

Heat through. Serve on hot rice. Top with garnish.

4 to 6 servings

VARIATIONS

◆ add sliced mushrooms; sauté with other mushrooms
◆ if time permits, slice tofu into strips 1 × 2 × ¼ inch; before adding, sauté until lightly browned and slightly crispy. Or follow the procedure for Batter-Dipped Tofu (p. 34).

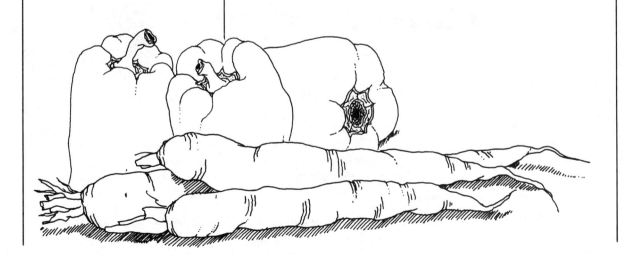

This is a light and colorful dish making the best use of fresh vegetables. Serve with rice or noodles and Mixed Fruit Chutney (p. 21) for a pleasing company meal.

ADVANCE PREPARATION

Vegetables may be sliced in advance, but further preparations are not recommended until just before serving.

VEGETABLE CURRY

3 to 4 cups hot cooked brown rice
1 cup cauliflower florets
2 carrots, sliced
1 cup broccoli florets
1 sweet red pepper, cut into 1 × ½-inch pieces
1 onion, cut into wedges
1 cup peas
2 tomatoes, cut into wedges

SAUCE
2 tablespoons safflower oil
2 tablespoons curry powder
2 tablespoons minced gingerroot
3 cloves garlic, minced
1 small red hot chili pepper, very finely chopped, or ¼ teaspoon dry crushed red pepper
½ cup vegetable stock
2 tablespoons lime juice

Garnish: *toasted sesame seeds, fresh coriander leaves, or roasted unsalted peanuts, optional*

HINT

♦ Curry powder is actually a blend of different herbs and spices, varying according to the country of origin. Varieties also vary in *intensity* of flavor, so add half the amount called for and then add more to taste. Also, the curry flavor becomes stronger in a dish that is allowed to stand or is kept refrigerated and then reheated.

Cook or reheat rice (see p. 14).

Steam cauliflower, carrots, and broccoli until crisp-tender, about 6 to 8 minutes. Add red pepper, onion, and peas for the last 3 minutes. Tomatoes should be added just for the last 2 minutes, simply to heat.

Meanwhile, in a small saucepan, heat oil for the sauce. Add curry powder, ginger, garlic, and chili pepper. Sauté for 3 to 5 minutes. Add vegetable stock and boil, uncovered, for about 3 minutes to reduce and thicken slightly. Stir in lime juice. Toss steamed vegetables gently with sauce. Top with garnish.

4 to 6 servings

VARIATIONS

♦ add 1 coarsely chopped apple
♦ add tofu cubes or serve on slices of lightly sautéed tofu. If time permits, follow the procedure for Batter-Dipped Tofu (p. 34)
♦ substitute or add other vegetables, such as sautéed mushrooms or steamed potatoes
♦ leftovers are delicious in omelets
♦ serve on buckwheat noodles or vermicelli, or other pasta

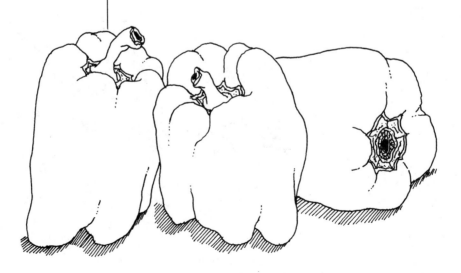

This is one of my favorite main courses for company. Chopping the vegetables in advance makes the last-minute stir-frying a snap. This dish is equally delicious when served on pasta, especially buckwheat noodles.

ADVANCE PREPARATION

For advance preparation of sauces, see individual recipes. For the stir-fry, vegetables may be chopped earlier in the day and refrigerated in tightly sealed bags. If possible, bring to room temperature before using. Cook just before serving.

VEGETABLE STIR-FRY WITH GINGER SAUCE

3 to 4 cups hot cooked brown rice
1 recipe Ginger Sauce (p. 28)
3 tablespoons safflower oil
2 carrots, thinly sliced diagonally
1 onion, thinly sliced
1 clove garlic, minced
4 stalks bok choy, sliced
1½ cups sliced mushrooms (4 ounces)
1 sweet red pepper, cut into strips
1 8-ounce can bamboo shoots, drained and rinsed
1 cup peas
½ pound firm tofu, cut into ½-inch cubes

Garnish: *toasted sesame seeds and unsalted peanuts, raw cashews, sliced almonds, mandarin orange sections, or scallion curls, optional*

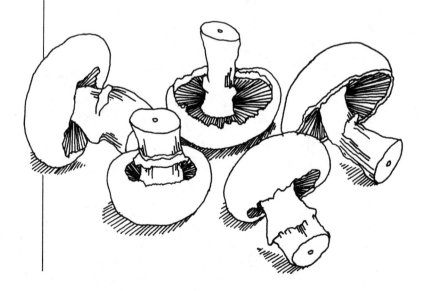

HINT

◆ When stir-frying vegetables, add them in order of hardness so that they will all be crisp-tender for serving.

Cook or reheat rice (see p. 14).

Cook Ginger Sauce; while it is simmering, assemble vegetables. Then cover sauce to keep it warm.

For the stir-fried vegetables, in a wok or large skillet, heat oil over medium-high heat. Add carrots; stir-fry for about 2 minutes. Add onion and garlic; continue to stir-fry for 2 more minutes. Add remaining ingredients except tofu. Stir-fry for about 4 more minutes, or until vegetables are heated through and are crisp-tender. Gently stir in tofu; cover pan, reduce heat, and allow to stand for about 1 minute.

To serve, dish out stir-fry mixture either onto individual beds of rice or onto a serving platter. Spoon on half of Ginger Sauce. Top with garnishes and serve immediately. Pass additional Ginger Sauce.

4 servings

VARIATIONS

◆ substitute or add other vegetables such as broccoli, baby corn ears, cucumber, water chestnuts, jicama, zucchini, bean sprouts, peapods, celery, tomato, napa cabbage—total should be 6 to 8 cups vegetables
◆ for the Ginger Sauce, substitute one of the following sauces: Garlic-Tomato (p. 25), Zesty Tomato (p. 26), Orange-Tahini (p. 27), Curry (p. 104), Tomato-Yogurt (p. 26), or Peanut (p. 28)
◆ chop all vegetables very finely, place tablespoon-size mounds on small lettuce leaves, add sauce, garnish with a small, thin strip of sweet red pepper, and serve as an appetizer

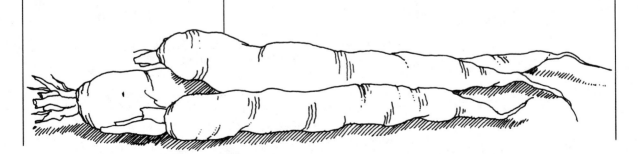

This is a delicious main course for spring when you want to make the most of the asparagus season.

ADVANCE PREPARATION

Vegetables may be chopped in advance, but advance cooking is not recommended for best quality.

ASPARAGUS-CASHEW STIR-FRY

3 to 4 cups hot cooked brown rice

SAUCE
3 tablespoons soy sauce
2 tablespoons cornstarch
1½ cups water or vegetable stock
1 tablespoon minced gingerroot
1 teaspoon sesame oil, preferably toasted sesame oil
¼ teaspoon dry crushed red pepper, or more to taste
dash of white pepper

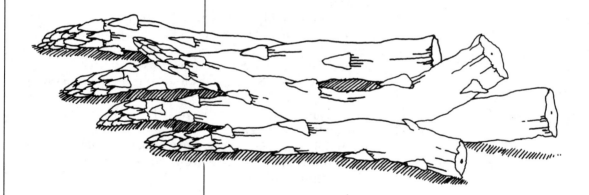

2 tablespoons safflower oil
1 pound fresh asparagus, woody parts of stems removed, tender part cut into 3-inch lengths (about 3 cups)
4 scallions, chopped
1 small sweet red pepper, chopped
1 clove garlic, minced
1 cup cashews, dry-roasted and unsalted or raw, or slivered almonds

HINTS

◆ Dried green herbs will keep a long time if tightly covered in a dark, cool cabinet. They lose flavor as they get old, however, so sometimes you may need to add more than a recipe calls for. Red herbs, such as crushed red pepper and curry powder, tend to lose or change flavor over time. It is a good idea to replace them after a year of storage.

◆ Tofu and cashews contain complementary amino acids, and thus will form high-quality complete protein.

◆ The best method I have found for keeping gingerroot on hand is to wrap the entire root in aluminum foil and keep it in the freezer. Peel the end and grate with a fine grater as needed. Frozen, the gingerroot will keep for months and is always there when you need it. At room temperature, ginger will keep for 1 month; refrigerated, it keeps only about 1 week. Chunks of the root can be refrigerated in a jar filled with dry sherry; it will keep for months.

Garnish: *mandarin orange sections and toasted sesame seeds, optional*

Cook or reheat brown rice (see p. 14).

In a small bowl, combine soy sauce and cornstarch. Stir in remaining sauce ingredients; set aside.

In a wok or large skillet, heat oil. Stir-fry asparagus, scallions, pepper, and garlic until vegetables are crisp-tender.

Stir sauce mixture; pour it over the vegetables and stir until it is thickened and bubbly. Reduce heat; fold in cashews. Cover and cook for 1 minute, until cashews are heated through.

Serve over rice. Top with garnishes.

4 servings

VARIATIONS

◆ 3 to 4 cups broccoli florets may be substituted for the asparagus; or add other vegetables such as sliced mushrooms or thinly sliced carrots

◆ with the cashews, gently stir in 1 pound firm tofu cut into ½-inch cubes

◆ serve over pasta rather than rice; buckwheat noodles are especially good

OMELET FILLING AND SAUCE COMBINATIONS

Omelets are simple creations that may be dressed up or varied by using different fillings and sauces. The following are some of my favorite combinations. Use them with your choice of the Noodle Omelet (see following recipe), French Omelet (p. 18), or Fluffy Omelet (p. 122).

This is a very simple dish that may be dressed up or varied by using different fillings and sauces.

ADVANCE PREPARATION
The omelet should be prepared just before serving.

HINTS
◆ Using only egg whites does not reduce the protein content of egg dishes. In fact, egg whites are considered the highest quality protein.
◆ Turmeric is the main ingredient in natural yellow food coloring available in many health food stores and can be added sparingly to egg whites to give them an egglike appearance.

NOODLE OMELET

½ cup fine egg noodles
6 eggs
3 tablespoons cold water
filling and sauce (see following recipes)
2 tablespoons margarine

Boil a pot of water; cook noodles until *al dente*.

Meanwhile, beat eggs and water together. When noodles are cooked, drain well. Add noodles to egg mixture and combine thoroughly. Prepare your choice of filling and sauce.

In a large skillet, heat margarine. Pour in egg mixture. As the edges become firm, lift them to allow egg to run out to the sides.

While egg is still moist, spread the center third with the filling perpendicular to the handle of the pan. Using a spatula, turn the third closest to the noodles to cover the filling. Cover the pan and heat over low for about 2 minutes, just to heat the filling.

Turn the omelet onto a serving platter by sliding the outermost third onto the platter and rolling the remainder over so that the omelet rests, seam side down, on the platter.

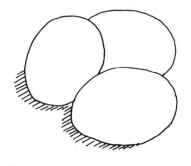

Spoon warm sauce over the omelet; garnish; cut into quarters to serve.

4 servings

VARIATIONS

◆ substitute 12 egg whites, plus 1½ tablespoons safflower oil and a dash of turmeric, for eggs, or use fewer yolks and replace them with extra whites (using only egg whites does not reduce the protein content of dishes)
◆ substitute cooked rice for noodles
◆ omit noodles for a plain omelet

ADVANCE PREPARATION

Filling can be made 1 day in advance. Bring to room temperature.

TOMATO-RICOTTA OMELET

Herbed Tomato Sauce (p. 75)

RICOTTA FILLING

¾ cup ricotta cheese, part skim variety
1 tablespoon low-fat milk
1 teaspoon fresh chopped parsley
1 teaspoon tarragon
¼ teaspoon black pepper

Garnish: *sautéed pine nuts, fresh basil leaves, Parmesan cheese, or steamed asparagus tips, optional*

In a small bowl, mix filling ingredients.

Fill omelet with Ricotta Filling. Cover to heat for 1 or 2 minutes. Turn out onto serving dish. Top with Herbed Tomato Sauce; garnish.

VARIATION

◆ substitute cottage cheese for all or part of the ricotta cheese; eliminate milk

ADVANCE PREPARATION

Sauce can be made 1 day in advance. Refrigerate; reheat to serve. Bring chutney to room temperature before assembling omelet.

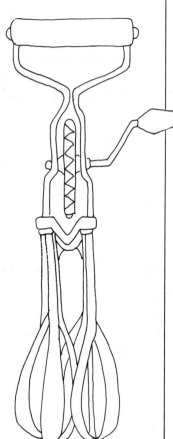

CURRY-CHUTNEY OMELET

CURRY SAUCE

2 tablespoons margarine
1 cup sliced mushrooms
1 carrot, grated
2 tablespoons chopped onion
1 tablespoon curry powder
¼ teaspoon black pepper
⅛ teaspoon ground cumin
1 cup low-fat milk
¼ cup apple juice
1 tablespoon cornstarch

6 tablespoons Mixed Fruit Chutney (p. 21)

Garnish: *fresh parsley sprigs, fresh coriander leaves, or currants, optional*

In a medium-size saucepan, heat margarine; sauté mushrooms, carrot, onion, and curry powder until onion is tender. Stir in pepper, cumin, and milk; simmer for 3 minutes, stirring occasionally.

In a measuring cup, combine apple juice and cornstarch; mix well. Stir into curry mixture; cook over medium heat, stirring constantly, until just thickened, about 5 minutes.

Fill omelet with Mixed Fruit Chutney. Top with Curry Sauce; garnish.

VARIATIONS

♦ add 1 cup baby peas
♦ use less curry powder if you do not like your food too hot

TOMATO-PESTO OMELET

Herbed Tomato Sauce (p. 75)
Pesto or Spinach-Parsley Pesto (pp. 22–23)

Garnish: *fresh basil sprigs or pine nuts*

Fill omelet with your choice of pesto. Top with Herbed Tomato Sauce; garnish.

OTHER OMELET IDEAS

Fill your omelet with chopped, steamed, or sautéed vegetables and top with one of the following sauces:

- ◆ Garlic-Tomato Sauce (p. 25)
- ◆ Tomato-Yogurt Sauce (p.26)
- ◆ Zesty Tomato Sauce (p. 26)
- ◆ Ginger Sauce (p. 28)

Remember that omelets are an ideal use for leftover pasta toppings or stir-fry dishes.

Simple yet delicious, this is what 15-minute cooking is all about!

ADVANCE PREPARATION

Tomato Hot Sauce may be mixed in advance and heated at serving time. Guacamole Filling is best made just before serving. Omelet should be made just before serving.

HINT

◆ Ripe avocados are soft fleshed under the skin. The skin may be speckled with brown or even all brown as long as the avocado does not feel mushy.

GUACAMOLE OMELET WITH TOMATO HOT SAUCE

TOMATO HOT SAUCE
1 15-ounce can unsalted tomato sauce (2 cups)
¼ teaspoon hot pepper sauce
1 teaspoon ground coriander
½ teaspoon black pepper
¼ teaspoon ground cumin
dash of crushed red pepper, optional

GUACAMOLE FILLING
2 avocados, at room temperature
3 tablespoons plain yogurt
2 tablespoons lemon juice or lime juice
1 tablespoon chopped onion
dash of hot pepper sauce
dash of freshly ground black pepper

8 eggs
4 tablespoons cold water
2 tablespoons margarine

Garnish: *tomato slices, alfalfa sprouts, parsley, orange wedges, dollop of plain yogurt, grated Cheddar or Monterey jack cheese, optional*

For the sauce, in a small saucepan, combine sauce ingredients; cover and simmer over low heat.

Meanwhile, for the filling, peel and halve avocados. Place in a food processor fitted with steel blade along with remaining filling ingredients. Process until smooth (or if you prefer, process only until partially smooth, leaving filling somewhat chunky). Cover and set aside.

For the omelet, in a medium-size bowl, beat eggs with water. In a large skillet, heat margarine over medium heat. Pour in egg mixture; stir with a fork, tilting the pan occasionally so uncooked eggs can flow to the bottom. While the top still looks moist and creamy, spread avocado mixture down the center of omelet. Fold the two edges of the omelet over, reduce heat to low, and allow to heat for 1 minute.

Slice into 4 portions; remove each with a spatula.

Pour about ¼ cup Tomato Hot Sauce over each serving. Top with one or a combination of the suggested garnishes.

4 servings

VARIATIONS

- ◆ use only 1 avocado; add ¼ to ½ cup tofu to the filling ingredients before pureeing
- ◆ use Guacamole Filling as a dip for taco chips, Pita Crisps (p. 52), or raw vegetables
- ◆ substitute 16 egg whites plus 2 tablespoons safflower oil and a dash of turmeric for eggs, or use fewer yolks and replace them with extra whites

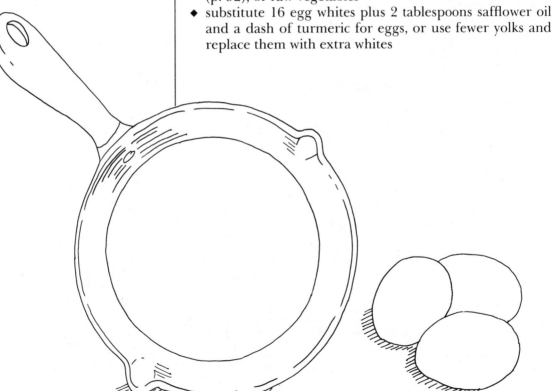

Prepare in an attractive skillet that can be used for presentation. When time permits, serve it topped with Marinara Sauce (p. 24); Garlic-Tomato Sauce (p. 25); or Tomato-Yogurt Sauce (p. 26). Curried Fruit (p. 125) makes an ideal side dish.

ADVANCE PREPARATION

Sauces may be prepared in advance according to individual recipes. Vegetables for the omelet may be chopped in advance, but omelet should be cooked just before serving (unless you plan to serve it chilled as an appetizer).

ITALIAN GARDEN FRITTATA

3 tablespoons margarine
1 cup sliced fresh mushrooms (3 ounces)
1 cup sliced zucchini
½ sweet red pepper, cut into julienne strips
½ green bell pepper, cut into julienne strips
1 scallion, chopped
1 clove garlic, minced
4 eggs, lightly beaten
¾ cup freshly grated Parmesan cheese, divided (3 ounces)
dash of freshly ground black pepper
3 tablespoons water
dash of basil
dash of oregano

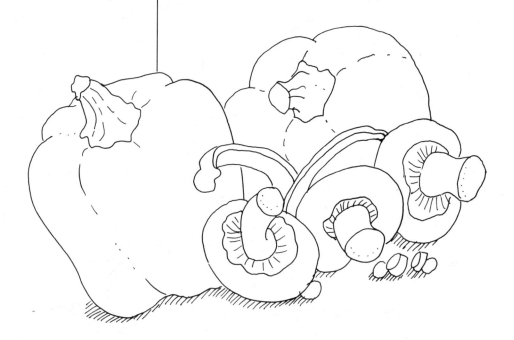

HINTS

◆ Whenever possible, cook vegetables with skins on. Vitamins stored just below the skin may be lost in peeling

◆ Never soak vegetables in water before cooking or you may lose water-soluble nutrients.

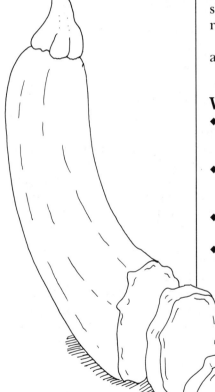

Garnish: *sliced sautéed mushrooms and paprika, optional*

In a large skillet, heat margarine over medium heat. Add mushrooms, zucchini, peppers, scallion, and garlic. Sauté, stirring occasionally, until vegetables are tender, about 5 minutes.

Meanwhile, in a medium-size bowl, combine eggs with ¼ cup of the Parmesan cheese. Add remaining seasonings and water. Pour mixture over cooked vegetables. Tilt pan cover over the pan, allowing the steam to escape. Cook over medium heat until eggs are set, 6 to 8 minutes. Serve from skillet or loosen around edges with a rubber spatula and slide onto serving plate (warm if possible). Sprinkle with remaining Parmesan cheese.

Slice into wedges, garnish with mushrooms and paprika, and serve immediately.

4 servings

VARIATIONS

◆ substitute or add other vegetables such as shredded carrots, sliced potatoes, peas, tomato, asparagus, or broccoli florets

◆ substitute 8 egg whites plus 1 tablespoon safflower oil and a dash of turmeric for the whole eggs—or use fewer yolks and replace them with extra whites

◆ use an oven-proof skillet; just before eggs are set, place pan under oven broiler to brown the top of the frittata

◆ to use as an appetizer, finely chop the vegetables. Cut frittata into thin wedges or cubes. Serve warm or at room temperature accompanied by Herbed Tomato Sauce (p. 75).

With eggs and tofu or nuts, this dish contains enough protein to stand alone. I like to serve steamed broccoli or asparagus as an accompaniment.

ADVANCE PREPARATION

May be made in advance; reheats well.

HINT

◆ Do not wash fresh mushrooms prior to storing them in the refrigerator and do not store them in a tightly sealed container or bag. Before using them, simply brush them or wipe with a moist paper towel. This vegetable is very absorbent and should not be allowed to soak in water.

ORIENTAL STIR-FRIED RICE

3 tablespoons safflower oil, divided
2 eggs, beaten
1 cup sliced mushrooms (3 ounces)
1 stalk celery, chopped
½ cup bean sprouts
½ cup alfalfa sprouts
2 scallions, chopped
2 cups cooked brown rice
1 cup peas
2 tablespoons soy sauce
dash of white pepper

Garnish: *sweet red pepper strips, optional*

In a wok or skillet, heat 1 tablespoon of the oil. Reduce heat to medium and add eggs. Scramble until eggs are almost set; remove from pan and set aside.

In the same pan, heat remaining oil. Add mushrooms, celery, sprouts, and scallions; stir-fry for about 2 minutes. Add rice; fry for 3 to 5 minutes. Continue stirring and add peas, soy sauce, pepper, and reserved eggs. Cook until heated through. Garnish with sweet red pepper strips.

4 servings

VARIATIONS

◆ substitute 4 egg whites for 2 eggs
◆ add ¼ to ½ pound firm tofu, cubed. Stir in with reserved eggs and heat through.
◆ add slivered almonds or raw cashews; stir-fry with vegetables to lightly brown

This is an ideal one-dish meal incorporating stir-fried vegetables, rice, and egg. All of the chopping can be done in your food processor to speed up preparations. I like to serve it with a spinach-mushroom salad with Honey-Poppyseed Dressing (p. 57).

ADVANCE PREPARATION
Vegetables can be chopped in advance; cook just before serving.

HINTS
◆ Bok choy is a vegetable that resembles Swiss chard in shape but is lighter in color and flavor. It can be found in most supermarket produce sections. Select crisp, unblemished stalks with bright, unwilted leaves.
◆ Jicama, like water chestnuts, will stay crisp when cooked.

ORIENTAL RICE AND VEGETABLE SKILLET

2 tablespoons safflower oil
1 medium-size onion, finely chopped (1/2 cup)
1 carrot, chopped
2 stalks bok choy, chopped (including leaves)
1/2 sweet red pepper, chopped
1 cup peapods, strings removed (about 4 ounces)
1 cup fresh bean sprouts
1 cup shredded spinach leaves
2 cups cooked brown rice
1/4 cup slivered almonds (1 ounce)
2 tablespoons soy sauce
1/2 teaspoon black pepper
2 eggs, lightly beaten

Garnish: *toasted sesame seeds, optional*

In a large skillet, heat oil. Add onion and carrot; stir-fry until onion is tender. Add bok choy, red pepper, peapods, bean sprouts, and spinach as they are prepared. Cook until spinach is wilted and other vegetables are crisp-tender, 3 to 5 minutes. Stir in rice, almonds, soy sauce, and pepper. Stir in eggs; cook, stirring constantly, for about 4 minutes, until lightly set. Garnish with toasted sesame seeds.
    4 servings

VARIATIONS
◆ add or substitute other vegetables such as mushrooms, jicama, green bell pepper, or peas
◆ substitute cooked noodles such as buckwheat noodles or Chinese noodles for rice
◆ substitute 3 or 4 egg whites for eggs

This is a nice easygoing dish because if necessary you can keep it warm in a covered skillet. The almonds, cheeses, and rice provide a complete protein.

ADVANCE PREPARATION

The recipe should be prepared just before serving, but it will hold well in a covered skillet.

HINTS

◆ Rice, bulgur wheat, and other cereal grains should be cooked until *al dente* so as not to be mushy.

◆ Many supermarkets have salad bars; if you are in a hurry, you can purchase the chopped vegetables to use in main courses and soups.

CHEF'S GARDEN SKILLET

2 cups broccoli florets
2 carrots, thinly sliced
2 small zucchini, sliced
½ cup peas
1 cup ricotta cheese, preferably part skim variety
2 tablespoons grated Parmesan cheese
1 tablespoon margarine
1 clove garlic, minced
1 small onion, chopped (¼ cup)
¼ cup slivered almonds (1 ounce)
2 cups cooked rice
1 tablespoon soy sauce
1 8-ounce can unsalted tomato sauce (1 cup)
1 teaspoon oregano
1 tablespoon chopped fresh parsley
½ teaspoon black pepper
1 cup shredded mozzarella cheese (4 ounces)
dash of paprika

Steam vegetables until crisp-tender.

Meanwhile, in a small bowl, stir ricotta and Parmesan cheese together. Set aside.

In a large, deep-sided skillet, melt margarine. Add garlic, onion, and almonds. Sauté, stirring occasionally, until onion is tender and almonds are lightly browned. Stir in rice and soy sauce. Smooth out the top of mixture. Drop on spoonfuls of ricotta mixture.

In a large bowl, combine steamed vegetables with tomato sauce, oregano, parsley, and pepper. Spread over ricotta layer in the skillet.

Top with shredded mozzarella cheese and sprinkle with paprika. Cover and heat for about 5 minutes, until cheese is melted.

6 servings

Mexican dishes adapt well to meatless versions. If served with refried beans, the taco shells and beans will combine to form a complete protein. I usually set the taco filling and condiments in a buffet and allow family or guests to assemble their own.

ADVANCE PREPARATION

Taco filling may be prepared in advance and reheated. Assemble tacos just before serving.

HINT

◆ Store hot pepper sauce in the refrigerator to prevent it from darkening in color and to retain its flavor.

VARIATIONS

◆ substitute or add other vegetables such as red cabbage, green beans, or onion
◆ combine wheat germ or bran with shredded cheese before adding as a topping

VEGETARIAN TACOS

2 tablespoons safflower oil
1 clove garlic, minced
1 small onion, chopped (¼ cup)
2 zucchini, sliced
3 cups sliced mushrooms (8 ounces)
1 carrot, shredded
2 tomatoes, cubed
1 8-ounce can tomato sauce (1 cup)
1 tablespoon chili powder
¼ teaspoon ground cumin
dash of hot pepper sauce
8 taco shells
2 cups shredded Cheddar cheese (½ pound)
¼ head lettuce, shredded
taco hot sauce (optional)

Garnish: *orange sections and alfalfa sprouts, optional*

Preheat oven to 350° F.

In a large skillet, heat oil. Stir in garlic, onion, zucchini, mushrooms, and carrot. Toss until zucchini is crisp-tender. about 4 minutes. Stir in ¾ of the cubed tomatoes, tomato sauce, chili powder, cumin, and hot pepper sauce. Cover and simmer for about 5 minutes.

Meanwhile, place taco shells on a baking sheet and warm in the oven for about 5 minutes.

To serve, spoon vegetable mixture into taco shells. Add cheese, lettuce, and remaining tomato. Top with a dash of

taco sauce. Garnish plates with orange sections and alfalfa sprouts.

4 to 6 servings

VARIATIONS

◆ add beans such as kidney beans or garbanzo beans to the taco filling
◆ make your own taco hot sauce using the Tomato Hot Sauce recipe on page 106
◆ rather than using taco shells, use the Veggy Taco mixture
  —as an omelet filling
  —as a pita bread filling
  —as a topping for English muffins: toast muffin halves first, spread on topping, top with cheese, and place under broiler for a few minutes to melt cheese

As an alternative to rice, couscous is tasty and requires only minutes to prepare. Here it is used as a main course, but leftover couscous can be used in salads.

ADVANCE PREPARATION

The sauce may be prepared in advance and reheated. Prepare couscous and assemble the recipe just before serving.

COUSCOUS WITH EGG SAUCE AND GARDEN VEGETABLES

4 cups chopped broccoli

EGG SAUCE
2 hard- or soft-cooked eggs
1 1/2 cups milk
3 tablespoons margarine
1 clove garlic, minced
3 tablespoons unbleached flour
2 tablespoons minced fresh parsley
1/4 teaspoon mustard powder
2 teaspoons soy sauce
white pepper, to taste

1 1/2 cups vegetable stock or water
1 1/2 cups dry couscous (1/2 pound)

Garnish: *dash of paprika, optional*

HINT

◆ Couscous is a wheat product made by forming tiny pellets from a mixture of flour and water. When prepared, it will double in volume. It is usually available in grocery stores and health food stores.

Steam broccoli.

While broccoli is cooking, in a blender or food processor, process eggs and milk until smooth; set aside.

In a saucepan, melt margarine, sauté garlic until softened, and stir in flour. Reduce heat and cook, stirring constantly, for 1 minute. Remove from heat; gradually stir in egg and milk mixture. Add remaining sauce ingredients and heat through.

Meanwhile, heat stock or water; in a medium-size bowl, stir together dry couscous and stock or water. Let stand, covered, until liquid is completely absorbed, about 5 to 10 minutes. Toss lightly.

For each serving, spoon broccoli over a mound of couscous. Cover with sauce. Garnish with paprika.

4 servings

VARIATIONS

◆ substitute other vegetables for the broccoli such as a combination of sautéed sliced red pepper, zucchini, and onion
◆ serve with Zesty Tomato Sauce (p. 26)
◆ use Egg Sauce as a topper for steamed vegetables

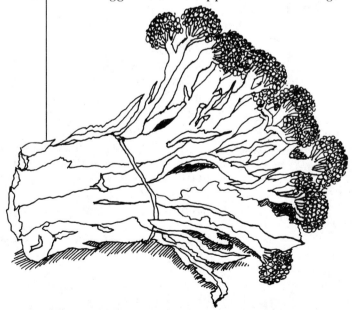

This is often my husband's choice when I ask what he would like for dinner. Savory Nut Burgers can be served on buns with lettuce, tomato slices, melted cheese, and ketchup, as well as with your choice of the suggested sauces.

ADVANCE PREPARATION

The Savory Nut Burger mixture can be mixed in advance; cook the patties just before serving.

HINTS

◆ Raw unroasted nuts are the healthiest. Roasting destroys some vitamins and enzymes and often adds fat.
◆ The addition of beaten eggs produces lightness in a mixture. Unbeaten eggs make ingredients adhere to one another.

SAVORY NUT BURGERS

1 egg or 2 egg whites
1 cup finely chopped walnuts, raw cashews, or almonds
¼ cup cottage cheese
½ cup toasted wheat germ, whole wheat bread crumbs, or crushed crackers
1 clove garlic, minced
2 tablespoons sesame seeds
1 tablespooon chopped fresh parsley
1 tablespoon chopped onion
1 teaspoon soy sauce
¼ teaspoon thyme leaves
¼ cup milk
1 tablespoon safflower oil

In a medium-size mixing bowl, combine ingredients except oil; mix well. Form mixture into 4 patties, each ½ inch thick.

In a large skillet, heat oil. Cook patties over medium heat on both sides until lightly browned, about 2 minutes on each side.

4 servings

VARIATIONS

◆ serve Savory Nut Burgers with one of the following sauces: Garlic-Tomato (p. 25), Zesty Tomato (p. 26), Tomato-Yogurt (p. 26), Curry (p. 104), Peanut (p. 28)
◆ make Sloppy Joes by omitting the bread crumbs or cracker crumbs. Sauté mixture in skillet until lightly browned. Stir in ½ cup tomato sauce; heat. May be served alone, in buns, or stuffed into pita bread.
◆ make Nut Balls to serve as appetizers. Form the mixture into walnut-sized balls. Either sauté lightly or bake on a baking sheet at 350° F. for about 8 minutes until lightly browned. Serve warm with Tomato-Yogurt Sauce (p. 26), Zesty Tomato Sauce (p. 26), or Peanut Sauce (p. 28).

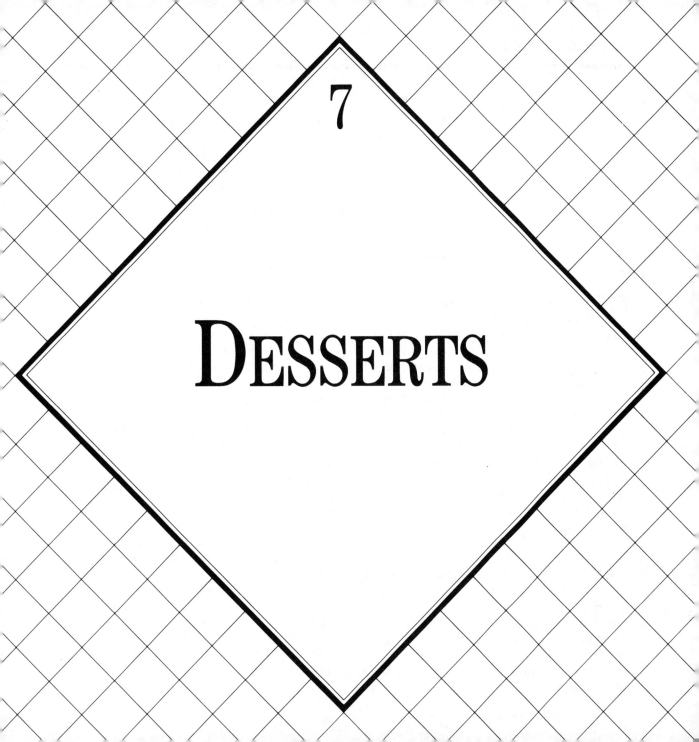

7

DESSERTS

These 15-minute finales do not taste as if they were prepared hastily. They are simple and light, but elegant and satisfying. And even though most of the recipes use little or no sugar, limited quantities of oil or margarine, low-fat milk products, and fewer eggs, I guarantee delicious results. Those recipes that contain chocolate and sugar are great for special occasions. After all, to many people, an indulgent dessert *is* the best part of the meal. Fruit is the simplest and healthiest of all desserts. Serve the freshest in-season fruit with a fabulous sauce and no one will know just how easy it was to prepare.

Or serve sliced fresh fruit without sauce, but give it extra pizzazz by adding a hint of spice. Try fresh pears sprinkled with ginger or add a dash of cinnamon or nutmeg to sliced tart apples. Squeeze some fresh lime juice over any kind of melon. None of these extra touches will take you more than a minute.

The only thing you must remember about fresh fruit is that it must be fully ripe when it is served because most fruits are not at their sweetest until they are fully ripe. Fruit ripening bowls are a worthwhile purchase, readily available in many gourmet shops and supermarkets. These clear-plastic bowls with domed, vented lids ripen "supermarket-hard" fruits to their optimum sweetness.

Cooking fruit gives it a different taste and texture, and makes it a marvelous base for a variety of sauces. Frozen fruit can be used to make sorbets, which are fast becoming one of America's most popular light desserts. Frozen bananas have a rich, smooth texture, like ice cream without the fat. I like to keep frozen fruit in the freezer at all times for healthy snacks and speedy desserts.

Much of the pleasure of dessert is visual, so make sure to go all out for dessert presentation. Even the simplest dessert can look like a fantastic creation if it is served in the right dish or goblet and elegantly garnished.

Poached pears are pretty and delicious on their own, but Maple Hot Chocolate Sauce (p. 134) will make them memorable. This dessert can be served warm or chilled.

ADVANCE PREPARATION

To serve warm, poach pears and serve immediately. To serve chilled, poach pears in advance, cover, and refrigerate for 4 to 6 hours.

HINTS

◆ When you peel pears for cooking, treat them like apples. To keep them from discoloring, as soon as they are peeled, drop them into water containing 1 tablespoon lemon juice.

◆ Poaching time will depend on the ripeness of the pears. It is best to begin with room-temperature pears that are ripe but still firm.

VANILLA POACHED PEARS

4 pears, at room temperature
2 tablespoons vanilla extract
2 tablespoons honey or maple syrup

Garnish: *chopped pecans, finely chopped or sliced almonds, toasted wheat germ, or fresh mint leaves, optional*

Half fill a Dutch oven or 3½- to 5-quart saucepan with water. Over high heat, bring to a boil.

Meanwhile, core and peel pears. Stir vanilla and honey into water. Set pears in water. Bring water back to a boil, reduce heat, and simmer until pears are tender but not soft, about 10 minutes (less if pears are quite ripe). Gently remove from poaching liquid. Serve with your choice of topping and garnish.

4 servings

VARIATIONS

◆ pears can be simply peeled and poached with stems intact
◆ substitute 1 cup orange juice for part of the poaching water, omitting the vanilla
◆ Carob Hot Fudge (p. 135), Honey-Raspberry Sauce (p. 136), or Orange-Raisin Sauce (p. 124) are also excellent served over or under the pears

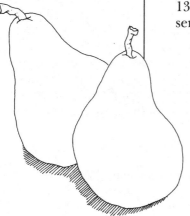

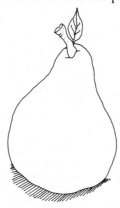

This low-fat yet elegant dessert may take a little more than fifteen minutes to prepare, but it will make a lasting impression on your guests. Though the final preparation must be done just before serving, it takes only minutes.

ADVANCE PREPARATION

Pears may be poached 1 to 2 hours ahead and allowed to come to room temperature. Fill, add meringue, and brown just before serving.

HINTS

◆ Egg whites at room temperature will have more volume when beaten. They also must be free of any yolk and the bowl should be totally clean of oil.
◆ Cream of tartar helps stabilize beaten egg whites, as does whipping the egg whites in an unlined copper bowl with a metal whisk.

POACHED PEARS ALASKA

4 Vanilla Poached Pears (preceding recipe)

FILLING
¼ cup almonds
¼ cup light raisins
2 tablespoons honey

MERINGUE
3 egg whites, at room temperature
⅛ teaspoon cream of tartar
½ cup sugar
¼ teaspoon vanilla extract

Garnish: *finely chopped pecans or toasted wheat germ, optional*

Poach pears. Allow to cool partially or come to room temperature.

Preheat oven to 450° F.

For the filling, place ingredients in bowl of a food processor fitted with steel blade. Process until blended together but not smooth. Stuff mixture into centers of pears.

For the meringue, beat egg whites with cream of tartar until soft peaks form. Continue beating, gradually adding sugar, about 1 tablespoon at a time; beat until peaks are stiff and glossy but mixture is not dry. Fold in vanilla.

With a rubber spatula, spread meringue over sides and tops of pears. Place pears on an ungreased baking sheet.

Bake pears in oven for 3 to 5 minutes, or until the meringue is lightly browned. Watch closely! Garnish each with finely chopped pecans or toasted wheat germ.

4 servings

VARIATION
◆ before serving, drizzle the pears lightly with Maple Hot Chocolate Sauce (p. 134), Carob Hot Fudge (p. 135), or Honey-Raspberry Sauce (p. 136)

This dessert provides a marvelous combination of tastes. If you do not have time to make your own chutney, many delicious commercially prepared varieties are available.

ADVANCE PREPARATION

The chutney may be made up to 2 weeks in advance. Bake the peaches just before serving if you plan to serve them warm; to serve at room temperature or chilled, they may be made earlier the same day.

HINT

◆ If peaches are not fragrant, they are not ripe. Avoid peaches with blemishes or shriveled skin.

BAKED PEACHES WITH CHUTNEY STUFFING

2 medium-size peaches, unpeeled, at room temperature
4 tablespoons Mixed Fruit Chutney (p. 21), at room temperature

Garnish: *finely chopped pecans or toasted wheat germ, optional*

Preheat oven to 350° F.

Halve peaches and remove pits.

Place peach halves on an ungreased baking sheet. Top each with 1 tablespoon chutney.

Bake in oven for 10 minutes, until peaches are tender and chutney is warm. Sprinkle with finely chopped pecans or toasted wheat germ and serve immediately.

4 servings

VARIATIONS

◆ substitute nectarines for peaches
◆ substitute canned peach halves, if necessary
◆ serve at room temperature or chilled

This is really something special—ideal for a snack or protein-rich dessert after a light meal; or consider serving it for a special brunch.

ADVANCE PREPARATION

◆ Omelet and sauce should be made just before serving.

HINT

◆ If you need eggs at room temperature and have forgotten to remove them from the refrigerator, place them in a pot of warm water for 10 minutes.

FLUFFY STRAWBERRY OMELET WITH NECTARINE SAUCE

4 eggs, separated
1 tablespoon powdered sugar
1 teaspoon vanilla extract
1 tablespoon margarine

NECTARINE SAUCE
1 large nectarine, peeled and quartered, at room temperature
2 tablespoons orange juice
1 tablespoon honey (the amount needed may vary according to sweetness of fruit)

1 cup sliced strawberries, at room temperature

Garnish: *kiwi slices, optional*

Preheat oven to 325° F.

In a small mixing bowl, using an electric mixer, beat egg whites until foamy. Add powdered sugar; continue beating until stiff peaks form.

In a separate bowl, beat egg yolks until thick and lemon-colored. Fold whites into yolks until well combined. Fold in vanilla.

In a large oven-proof skillet or one with a removable handle, melt margarine. Pour in egg mixture and cook for about 5 minutes, until bottom of omelet is lightly browned. Transfer pan to oven and bake for 5 to 6 minutes, until knife inserted in center comes out clean. Remove from oven.

While omelet is baking, place sauce ingredients in food processor. Blend until smooth.

Slide omelet onto serving platter; arrange strawberry slices over omelet. Pour on Nectarine Sauce. Cut into quarters to serve. Garnish with kiwi slices.

4 servings

This is a variation of the traditional dessert and probably one of the prettiest dishes you can serve.

ADVANCE PREPARATION

Honey-Raspberry Sauce may be prepared in advance and reheated; assemble this dessert just before serving.

HINTS

◆ Once peeled, peaches will turn brown quickly. If you do not plan to use them immediately, dip them in orange juice or lemon juice.

◆ To speed up peeling peaches, bring a pot of water to a boil and remove from heat. Immerse peaches in water for about 3 minutes; then peel.

VARIATIONS

◆ use beaten egg whites only and eliminate yolks—I call this Fruit on a Cloud, and it is delicious!
◆ if you do not have an oven-proof skillet, use 2 large spatulas to flip the omelet to brown the second side. This works best in a non-stick skillet.
◆ serve omelet with nectarine slices and top with Strawberry Sauce made by substituting 1 cup sliced strawberries for the nectarine
◆ use the Nectarine or Strawberry Sauce over chopped fruit, yogurt, or ice cream

PEACH MELBA

1 recipe Honey-Raspberry Sauce (p. 136)
2 medium-size peaches, peeled and halved, chilled or at room temperature
2 cups vanilla ice cream

Garnish: *almond slices or fresh mint leaves, optional*

Prepare Honey-Raspberry Sauce. Set aside to cool slightly.
   Place peach halves in dessert dishes. Top each with 1 scoop of ice cream. Spoon about ¼ cup warm Honey-Raspberry Sauce over each serving. Serve immediately, garnished with almond slices.
   4 servings

VARIATION

◆ substitute plain or vanilla yogurt for ice cream

If you are not in the habit of cooking bananas, you will be pleasantly surprised by their natural sweetness.

ADVANCE PREPARATION

The sauce and bananas will be at their best if made just before serving.

HINTS

◆ 1 banana contains 100 calories and is high in potassium.
◆ To squeeze more juice from lemons, limes, or oranges, microwave fruit 30 seconds on high before cutting and squeezing.

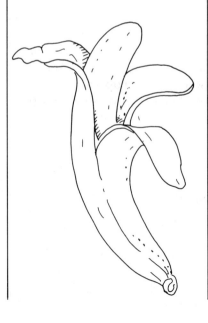

BROILED BANANAS WITH ORANGE-RAISIN SAUCE

ORANGE-RAISIN SAUCE
1¼ cups orange juice
1 tablespoon honey
1 tablespoon margarine
¼ cup raisins
1 tablespoon cornstarch
1 tablespoon water
dash of nutmeg

oil
4 bananas, at room temperature
2 teaspoons lemon juice
2 tablespoons margarine

Garnish: *chopped pecans, chopped walnuts, almond slices, or toasted wheat germ, optional*

In a saucepan, place orange juice, honey, margarine, and raisins. Bring to a simmer; reduce heat.

Preheat broiler.

Lightly oil a 9-inch square baking dish.

Peel bananas and cut them in half both lengthwise and crosswise. Arrange in prepared pan with uncut side up. Drizzle with lemon juice; dot with margarine. Place under broiler, about 5 inches from heating element. Broil for about 4 minutes, checking occasionally, until tender and lightly browned.

Meanwhile, in a measuring cup, combine cornstarch and cold water. Stir into Orange-Raisin Sauce. Simmer over low heat, stirring until thick, about 3 minutes. Stir in nutmeg.

To serve, place 4 banana sections in each of 4 individual bowls. Top with warm Orange-Raisin Sauce and garnish.

4 servings

◆

In addition to being one of my favorite desserts, this fruit dish is also excellent as a side dish.

ADVANCE PREPARATION
To serve warm, cook and serve immediately. Reheating may cause the fruits to become overcooked.

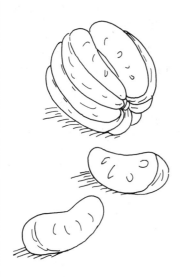

VARIATION
◆ serve Orange-Raisin Sauce on yogurt, vanilla ice cream, or poached fruit

CURRIED FRUIT

3 tablespoons margarine
¼ cup light brown sugar or 2 tablespoons honey
1 tablespoon curry powder
½ teaspoon ginger powder
1 8-ounce can pineapple chunks (canned in own juice), drained, reserving ¼ cup juice
1 11-ounce can mandarin oranges, drained
1 ripe pear, cut into 1-inch cubes, at room temperature
2 cups vanilla yogurt (16 ounces)

Garnish: chopped walnuts, chopped pecans, sunflower seeds, or mixture of ground nuts and finely grated orange rind, optional

In a medium-size saucepan, melt margarine. Add brown sugar, curry powder, and ginger. Cook, stirring occasionally over medium heat, for about 5 minutes, until sugar is melted and mixture is smooth.

Stir in fruit and ¼ cup pineapple juice; cover and cook for about 5 minutes, until fruit is heated through and pear chunks are tender.

Serve warm over yogurt. Top with garnish.
4 to 6 servings

VARIATIONS
◆ substitute or add other fresh fruit such as peaches, apricots, nectarines, and apples
◆ add about ¼ cup raisins
◆ serve chilled over ice cream

A simple and elegant dessert—one of my favorites in the fall when apples are at their best.

ADVANCE PREPARATION

The sauce may be made in advance and reheated, but the apples must be sautéed just before serving.

HINTS

◆ My favorite cooking apples are Rome Beauty. Others that cook well are Golden Delicious, Granny Smith, and Winesap. Avoid using Red Delicious and Jonathan, which are rather tender for cooking and lack the acidity that gives many dishes their characteristic flavor.

◆ When chopping or dicing dried fruit, coating the blade of the knife or kitchen shears with oil will make the task easier.

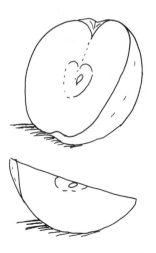

SAUTÉED APPLE SLICES WITH APRICOT-ORANGE SAUCE

APRICOT-ORANGE SAUCE   *makes ¹/₂ cup*
8 dried apricot halves
1 cup orange juice
¹/₄ teaspoon nutmeg

2 tablespoons unsalted margarine
1 tablespoon honey
1 teaspoon vanilla extract
¹/₄ cup sliced almonds
2 baking apples, peeled and cut into ¹/₄-inch slices, at room temperature

Garnish: *toasted wheat germ, optional*

To make the sauce, place apricots and orange juice in a medium-size saucepan. Bring to a boil; reduce heat to low, cover, and simmer until apricots are soft, about 10 minutes.

While apricots are cooking, in a large skillet over low heat, melt margarine. Stir in honey and vanilla. Add almond and apple slices. Increase heat to high, tossing almonds and apples for about 5 minutes, until apples are warmed through and tender but still crisp.

Pour apricot–orange juice mixture and nutmeg into a food processor; process until very smooth.

To serve, arrange apple slices and almonds on individual dessert plates. Top each with warm Apricot-Orange Sauce and toasted wheat germ. Serve immediately.
    4 servings

VARIATIONS

◆ substitute 4 dried peach halves for dried apricots
◆ substitute sliced pears for apples
◆ use sauce on plain yogurt, ice cream, pancakes, or over sliced fresh papaya

This is a showstopper—the flavors of pineapple, raspberry, and chocolate combine wonderfully.

ADVANCE PREPARATION

The chocolate-dipped fruit may be prepared several hours in advance; see sauce recipe for advance sauce preparation. Assemble individual plates just before serving.

HINTS

◆ When dipping fruit in chocolate, make certain the fruit is completely dry.

◆ When a pineapple is ripe, the inner leaves at the crown come out easily; the skin is orange or yellow with no traces of green; the base of the fruit should smell sweet.

CHOCOLATE-DIPPED PINEAPPLE WITH HONEY-RASPBERRY SAUCE

1 large fresh pineapple, chilled
6 ounces semisweet chocolate
1 recipe Honey-Raspberry Sauce (p. 136)

Garnish: *fresh mint sprigs, optional*

Slice pineapple into discs ½ inch thick; remove peel.

In top of a double boiler, melt chocolate. While it is melting, line a baking sheet or shallow pan with wax paper.

Dip half of each pineapple ring into melted chocolate, easing excess chocolate off with a rubber spatula. Set pineapple on wax paper. When all fruit slices have been dipped, place in refrigerator.

Prepare Honey-Raspberry Sauce; allow to cool slightly.

To serve, pour a thin layer of Honey-Raspberry Sauce on individual dessert plates. Set on pineapple rings. Garnish with fresh mint sprigs and serve immediately.

6 servings

VARIATIONS

◆ in place of the pineapple, dip other fresh fruit into the chocolate—such as strawberries, grapes, or orange segments

◆ dried fruit and nuts, such as whole almonds in brown skins, can be dipped into the chocolate and can be used as part of a fruit platter or as a way to garnish a dessert

A light and elegant dessert—one of my favorites to serve after a spicy or rich entree. Even though the sauce contains not an ounce of sugar, honey, or other added sweeteners, it undoubtedly will satisfy your sweet tooth.

ADVANCE PREPARATION

The oranges may be made early the day they are to be served; cover and chill; serve cold.

HINT

◆ To easily remove the white membrane that clings to oranges, cover the unpeeled orange with boiling water, let stand for 5 minutes, then peel.

GLAZED ORANGES

4 oranges, at room temperature
6 ounces pineapple-orange juice concentrate, thawed
2 tablespoons lemon juice

Garnish: *fresh mint leaves, optional*

Zest the peel from 2 oranges. In a saucepan, place the zest and pineapple-orange juice. Bring to a boil, stirring constantly, until mixture reduces and darkens slightly, about 5 minutes. Remove from heat and stir in lemon juice. Allow to cool somewhat, about 5 minutes.

Meanwhile, peel remaining oranges. Place all 4 in serving dish. Pour glaze over fruit, placing mint leaves and a small amount of orange zest on each orange as a garnish.

Glazed Oranges can be served immediately, with the sauce warm, in shallow bowls with a knife and fork.

4 servings

VARIATIONS

◆ substitute pineapple juice concentrate for pineapple–orange juice concentrate
◆ if you prefer, slice the oranges or cut into wedges. If your guests will be eating on their laps rather than at a table, arrange in individual bowls and pour the sauce over.

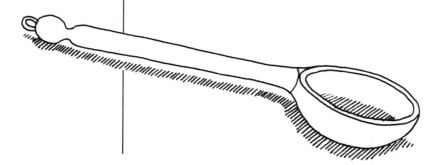

It is amazing how versatile ricotta cheese can be, not only as a main-course ingredient but also as the primary ingredient in this sensational dessert.

ADVANCE PREPARATION

Ricotta filling may be made several hours in advance. Slice pears in half and add filling just before serving.

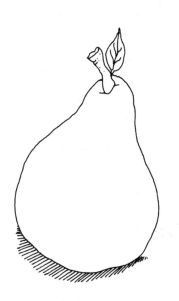

RICOTTA-TOPPED PEARS

1 cup ricotta cheese, part skim variety
2 tablespoons orange juice
1 tablespoon honey
¼ teaspoon almond extract
2 tablespoons slivered almonds
2 tablespoons carob chips or chocolate chips
2 tablespoons currants or chopped raisins
1 teaspoon grated orange rind
2 ripe pears, chilled or at room temperature

Garnish: *strawberries or raspberries, or sprinkle of carob cocoa powder, or chocolate cocoa powder, optional*

In a food processor, combine ricotta cheese, orange juice, honey, and almond extract until light and smooth. Stir in almonds, chips, currants or raisins, and orange rind.

Halve pears, placing one half in each of 4 individual bowls. For each serving, top fruit with about ¼ cup of the ricotta mixture and garnish.

4 servings

VARIATIONS

- ◆ substitute peaches for pears
- ◆ chop almonds and chocolate chips finely; stuff into dried fruit such as apricots, peaches, or prunes
- ◆ the ricotta topping may also be used as a filling for cannoli dessert shells (pastry tubes), which are often available at Italian delis or gourmet shops. Mixture will fill 4 shells. These can be filled up to 3 hours before serving.

If this sounds too easy to be good, I think you will be pleasantly surprised.

ADVANCE PREPARATION

May be made up to 1 day in advance if oranges are used. Must be served immediately if pears are substituted.

HINTS

◆ Color is not a sure guide to choosing oranges. Oranges that are heavy for their size and have relatively smooth skins will be the juiciest.

◆ Oranges are an excellent source of vitamin C.

MAPLE ORANGES AMANDINE

4 medium-size oranges, chilled
¼ cup orange juice
¼ cup maple syrup
¼ cup slivered almonds

Garnish: *fresh mint leaves, optional*

Peel oranges and cut into ½-inch cubes. Place in a medium-size bowl.

In a small bowl or cup, combine orange juice and maple syrup. Pour over oranges.

Divide oranges and syrup into 4 individual dessert bowls. Top each serving with almonds and garnish with fresh mint leaves.

4 servings

VARIATIONS

◆ substitute pears for oranges
◆ serve as a side dish for a brunch

Using frozen bananas is like magic, creating a dessert that tastes like the richest of ice creams without the calories and cholesterol.

ADVANCE PREPARATION

Bananas must be frozen in advance. Prepare the dessert just before serving.

HINT

◆ Yogurt originated when desert nomads carried goat's milk in bags on the backs of their camels. The heat turned it into yogurt!

FROZEN BANANA-BERRY PARFAITS

3 medium-size bananas
½ cup plain yogurt
2 tablespoons honey
1 cup sliced strawberries
1 cup blueberries

Garnish: *whole strawberries and grating of sweetened chocolate or carob, optional*

In advance, peel bananas, wrap in plastic bag, and freeze overnight.

At serving time, cut bananas into 1-inch slices while still frozen. Place yogurt and honey in food processor; process until combined. Gradually add banana slices; continue to process until smooth.

Spoon into parfait glasses, alternating with a layer of strawberries and a layer of blueberries. Top with garnishes and serve immediately.

4 servings

VARIATIONS

◆ add a dash of vanilla extract to the banana-yogurt mixture
◆ for a different flavor and a nice pink color, add strawberries (about 1 cup) as you are blending the mixture

I always keep some frozen fruit on hand for this recipe. It is a satisfying summer cooler and an ideal use for extra fruit on the verge of overripening.

ADVANCE PREPARATION
Fruit Smoothies are best served immediately; mixture may be placed in the freezer for 30 minutes before serving if necessary. Frozen longer, the mixture becomes quite icy.

HINT
◆ Frozen fruit is available without added sweeteners. Read the labels!

FRUIT SMOOTHIE

3 cups frozen mixed chopped fruit (cantaloupe, bananas, strawberries, peaches, or others of your choice)
1 cup apple juice or orange juice

Garnish: *kiwi slices, whole strawberries, or whole raspberries, optional*

Pour fruit and juice into a food processor or blender; blend until smooth, occasionally pushing down fruit chunks for uniform consistency. Top with garnish and serve immediately; mixture melts quickly!
makes 2 cups
4 to 6 servings

VARIATIONS
◆ substitute milk for apple juice; add 2 tablespoons sugar
◆ use individual frozen fruits rather than a mixture; strawberries are especially good

With a bit of advance planning, this dessert is one of the quickest I know.

ADVANCE PREPARATION

Pears must be frozen in advance. Dessert must be served immediately after being prepared.

PEAR SORBET

1 16-ounce can sliced pears, "lite" variety with no sugar added
¼ cup orange juice
1 tablespoon honey

Garnish: *strawberries, almond slices, or toasted wheat germ, optional*

In advance, drain pears and freeze in freezer container.

Ten minutes before serving, set container at room temperature to soften pears slightly.

Just before serving, place pears, orange juice, and honey in a food processor fitted with steel blade. Puree until smooth. Top with garnish and serve immediately. Leftover sorbet can be refrozen.

4 servings

VARIATIONS

◆ substitute 1½ 11-ounce cans mandarin oranges or 1 16-ounce can peaches (lite) for the pears
◆ for a creamier product, stir in some plain yogurt
◆ for a fluffier product, stir in 1 stiffly beaten egg white

DESSERT SAUCES

These are three of my favorite sauces, the finishing touch for some of the preceding deserts.

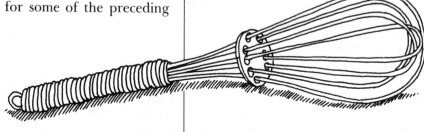

The flavors of chocolate and maple blend artfully to create a rich sauce ideal for special occasions. This sauce is a perfect topping for ice cream or frozen yogurt.

ADVANCE PREPARATION

This sauce will keep for about 1 week in the refrigerator. It will become very thick but can be reheated over boiling water.

HINTS

◆ In bottom pan of a double boiler, the water level should not touch the insert.

◆ Be sure to buy syrup labeled "pure maple syrup." Check labels for the addition of cornstarch, cane syrup, artificial maple flavor, and colorings. Once opened, maple syrup should be refrigerated.

MAPLE HOT CHOCOLATE SAUCE

4 ounces unsweetened chocolate
2 tablespoons unsalted margarine
¾ cup maple syrup
¼ cup milk

In bottom pan of a double boiler, heat water. Melt chocolate in top; then add and melt margarine. Stir in maple syrup and milk, stirring constantly as it heats. Pour into a food processor. Process until very smooth. Serve warm.
    makes 1 cup

VARIATIONS

◆ for maple syrup, substitute 1 cup sugar; add ¼ cup milk and 1 teaspoon vanilla extract. Cook, stirring, until sugar is dissolved.

◆ substitute ¾ cup honey for maple syrup

Carob has the advantages of being caffeine-free and low in fat. For variety, try it as an alternative to chocolate. This sauce is delicious on ice cream, frozen yogurt, and frozen tofu desserts.

ADVANCE PREPARATION

The sauce may be stored in the refrigerator for about 1 week and reheated to serve.

HINTS

◆ For best flavor, be sure to use real vanilla extract, not vanilla flavoring or artificial vanilla.

◆ Carob is high in fiber and calcium. About 3½ ounces of carob contains 180 calories; the same quantity of chocolate contains 520 calories.

CAROB HOT FUDGE

½ cup water
1 cup carob powder
1 egg
⅓ cup maple syrup
1 tablespoon unsalted margarine
2 teaspoons vanilla extract

In a saucepan, stir together water and carob powder until powder is dissolved. Bring to a boil, stirring constantly.

Beat egg lightly in a measuring cup. Stir in about ¼ cup of the hot carob mixture. Then pour back into pan while stirring. Add remaining ingredients and cook over low heat, stirring constantly, for about 5 minutes, until thick and smooth.

makes 1 cup

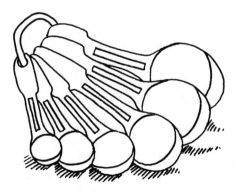

Keep frozen raspberries on hand to make this colorful sauce, which can be served on fruit, ice cream, or frozen yogurt.

ADVANCE PREPARATION

The sauce may be made 1 day in advance. After being chilled it may need to be thinned somewhat with water, apple juice, or orange juice.

HINTS

◆ As a rule, the lighter the color of honey, the milder its taste. If no flower source is listed on the label, the honey is a blend from several kinds of flowers.

◆ 2½ teaspoons arrowroot powder can be substituted for 1 tablespoon cornstarch.

HONEY-RASPBERRY SAUCE

2 cups frozen raspberries in "lite" sauce (10-ounce package)
2 tablespoons honey
1 tablespoon cornstarch
¼ cup water

In a small saucepan, combine raspberries and honey. Cook over low heat, stirring constantly, until just below boiling. Remove from heat.

In a measuring cup, mix cornstarch and water until smooth; add to honey-berry mixture. Stirring constantly, cook over low heat until thickened and smooth, about 5 minutes. Strain through a coarse sieve.

makes 1 cup

VARIATIONS

◆ substitute frozen strawberries for raspberries; do not strain
◆ substitute lime juice for water and increase honey to 3 tablespoons—it is delicious served on fresh papaya slices

8

The Vegetarian Entertainer

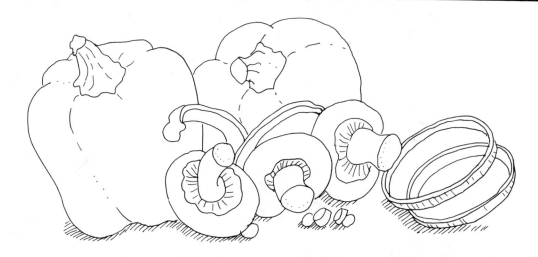

It might not take hours in the kitchen to produce a dinner party that comes off to perfection, but it does take careful thought. Here are some tips to keep in mind:

- Plan simple menus; they are usually best when cooking for more than 6. For small groups, serve in courses. For large groups, consider using a buffet setting.

- Never choose more than one recipe requiring last-minute attention.

- If some of your favorite party recipes are time-consuming, consider using one or more 15-minute recipes as accompaniments.

- Although most of my recipes were developed to serve from 4 to 6, many of them will adapt well for larger groups. This is relatively simple to do, though it may take longer than 15 minutes to prepare the adapted recipe. Keep in mind when adapting recipes that *you rarely need to increase herbs and other seasonings in the same proportion as the major ingredients.* Rule of thumb: When doubling a recipe, add 1½ times the amount of herbs.

- If you are preparing foods in advance, always refrigerate, bring to room temperature (time permitting), then reheat *just before serving.* Some of the more pungent seasonings such as curry powder and crushed red pepper will intensify in flavor as they set.

- Arrange your ingredients, equipment, and serving dishes so they are ready for instant action for last-minute preparations.

- I do not skimp on adornments; plan interesting table settings and add creative, colorful garnishes.

9

How to Plan a Vegetarian Meal

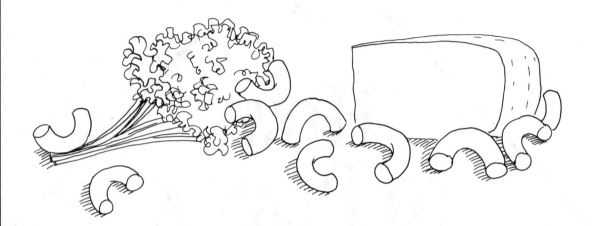

Many of the recipes in this book are meant to be a springboard for your own imagination. You might want to first try the original; then delve into the endless possibilities for variation, substitution, and innovation. Keep in mind that some of the suggested variations may require more preparation time, others less.

When you are planning a complete meal, remember:

- Always include a protein source in the meal. This may be as simple as serving tofu or eggs; also consult the complementary food combinations on pages 141 and 142.

- Do not repeat major ingredients in more than one course. For example, do not serve a tomato-based soup followed by a pasta with a tomato sauce.

- Take into account a variety of colors, textures, intensity of flavors, and a balance of raw and cooked foods.

- Check individual recipes for garnishes, variations, and advance preparation. Remember, nearly all of the recipes can be served immediately upon completion.

- Use leftovers creatively. Leftover pasta can be a rice or vegetable topping or an omelet filling. Using them is better than freezing them since the quality and texture of foods nearly always deteriorate after being frozen and thawed, thereby counteracting the advantages of using fresh ingredients in the first place.

- You can please the meat-eaters in your family by adding meat or serving meat with many of these recipes.

MENUS

Menu planning is the most important aspect of serving a really superb meal. I generally begin by selecting my main course and then choose accompaniments that will complement it in quality, flavor, or flamboyance.

The 15-minute main courses and many of the soups and salads can stand alone, but here are several points to serve as helpful guidelines for when you have more time or when the occasion demands a larger meal:

- variety: avoid repeating ingredients
- texture: balance creamy textures with crispness
- flavor: vary intensity of spices, and sweetness with tartness
- color: plan for variety; use brightly colored garnishes to offset blandly colored foods
- nutrition: include protein and a variety of nutrients
- weight: find a balance of rich and light foods
- season: use fresh, seasonal foods; lighter foods in hot weather, warming foods in cold weather
- complexity: for entertaining, select some do-ahead dishes so your party can be fun for you, too
- themes: for fun, carry out a theme in your food and table decor
- dietary restrictions and food preferences: please your family and guests with what suits them best

The menus that I have provided have earned me compliments from my family and friends.

SOUTHEAST ASIAN DINNER

Baba Ghannouj with Pita Crisps
Thai Cucumber Salad
Vegetable Curry with Brown Rice
Mixed Fruit Chutney
Broiled Bananas with Orange-Raisin Sauce

FALL LUNCHEON

Pureed Vegetable Soup with Broccoli
    Florets
Almond Butter–Wheat Germ Sticks
Sautéed Apple Slices with Apricot-Orange
    Sauce

COOL SUMMER SUPPER

Chunky Garden Gazpacho
Pita Crisps
Couscous· Currant Salad with Lemon
    Dressing
Frozen Banana-Berry Parfaits

LIGHT AND FRESH FEAST

Oriental Stew
Pasta with Chinese Tahini Sauce
Pear Sorbet

SIMPLE SOUP DINNER

Almond-Mushroom Pâté with crusty bread
Quick Pea Soup
Tossed Green Salad with Cherry Tomatoes,
    Cheese Cubes, and Honey-Poppyseed
    Dressing
Glazed Oranges

FAMILY DINNER

Savory Nut Burgers with Zesty Tomato Sauce
Steamed Asparagus
Rice and Spinach Salad with Oriental Vinaigrette
Baked Peaches with Chutney Stuffing

FESTIVE OMELET DINNER

Guacamole Omelet with Tomato Hot Sauce
Basil Bean Salad
Fruit Smoothie

MENU ITALIANO

Pasta Marinara on Beds of Spinach
Tossed Green Salad with Summer Peach Vinaigrette
Poached Pears Alaska with Maple Hot Chocolate Sauce

DO-AHEAD PARTY BUFFET

Pasta Salad Primavera with Herbed Tomato Sauce

Crusty French Bread with Pesto Herb Spread
Ricotta-Topped Pears (or filled cannoli shell variation)

MORNING GLORY BRUNCH

Italian Garden Frittata with Marinara Sauce
Assorted Breads and Muffins
Curried Fruit

STIR-FRY SPECIAL

Spinach and Strawberry Salad with Pepper Vinaigrette
Vegetable Stir-Fry with Ginger Sauce
Brown Rice
Chocolate-Dipped Pineapple with Honey-Raspberry Sauce

PASTA PICNIC

Pasta Shells with Lemon Vinaigrette
French Bread with Pesto Herb Spread
Maple Oranges Amandine

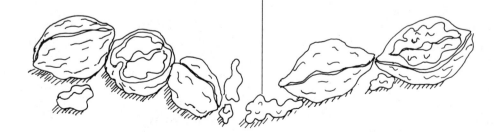

INDEX

Additives, 5
Advance planning, 6
    See also Planning meals
Almond
    butter–wheat germ sticks, 52–
        53
    -mushroom pâté, 30–31
Appetizers, 29–37
    almond-mushroom pâté, 30–
        31
    baba ghannouj, 31
    batter-dipped tofu, 34–35
    cheesy vegetable spread, 33
    curried cheese spread with
        chutney, 35
    curried yogurt dip, 37
    eggplant and sesame cream, 31
    hummus, 32
    peanut chili dip, 36
    suggested recipes, 37
Apple
    salad dressing, 59
    slices, sautéed with apricot-
        orange sauce, 126
Apricot-orange sauce, 126
Asparagus
    -cashew stir-fry, 100–01
    and pasta salad, 74–75

Baba ghannouj, 31
Baked peaches with chutney
    stuffing, 121
Balance in meals, 2–4
    carbohydrates and, 3
    dairy products and, 4
    fats and, 3
    protein and, 2–3
    raw and cooked foods, 4
    water and, 3–4
Banana(s)
    -berry parfaits, frozen, 131
    broiled, with orange-raisin
        sauce, 124–25
Basic foods, 11–28
    chutney, mixed fruits, 21
    condiments, 19–21
    grains, 14–15
    legumes, 17
    mayonnaise, 20
    mustard, 19
    omelets, 18
    pasta, 15–16
    pesto, 22–23
    sauces, 24–28
    vegetable stock, 12–13
Basil bean salad, 69
Basmati rice, 14

Batter-dipped tofu, 34–35
Bean salad, basil, 69
Blenders, 7
Blueberry soup, 50
Broiled bananas with orange-
    raisin sauce, 124–25
Broiling, 8
Bulgur wheat, 15

Calcium, 4
Carbohydrates, 3
    complex, 3
    simple, 3
Carob hot fudge (sauce), 135
Carrot soup, 45
Cheese
    -poppyseed noodles, 91
    spread, curried with chutney, 35
Cheesy vegetable spread, 33
Chef's garden skillet, 112–13
Chick pea
    hummus, 32
    soup, 47
    -zucchini curry, 87
Chili (meatless mission soup), 42
Chinese tahini sauce, 88
Chocolate-dipped pineapple with
    honey-raspberry sauce, 127

Chopping by hand, 8
Chunky garden gazpacho, 48
Chutney, mixed fruit, 21
    dressing, 60
Cold-pressed oils, 10
Cold-tossing, 8
Complex carbohydrates, 3
Condiments, 19–21
    chutney, mixed fruit, 21
    mayonnaise, 20
    mustard, 19
Cool summer supper menu, 141
Couscous, 15
    -currant salad with lemon
        dressing, 72–73
    with egg sauce and garden
        vegetables, 114–15
Creamy Italian dressing, 76
Croutons, herbed garlic, 51
Cucumber salad, 65
Curried cheese spread with
    chutney, 35
Curried fruit, 125
Curried yogurt dip, 37
Curried yogurt dressing, 62
Curry-chutney omelet, 104

Dairy products, 4
    calcium and, 4
    as protein source, 4
Desserts, 117–36
    apple slices, sautéed with
        apricot-orange sauce, 126
    banana(s)
        -berry parfaits, frozen, 131
        broiled, with orange-raisin
            sauce, 124–25
    carob hot fudge (sauce), 135
    curried fruit, 125
    fruit, 118
        smoothie, 132
    honey-raspberry sauce, 136
    maple hot chocolate sauce, 134
    orange(s)
        glazed, 128
        maple, amandine, 130

peach(es)
    baked, with chutney stuffing,
        121
    Melba, 123
pear(s)
    poached Alaska, 120
    ricotta-topped, 129
    sorbet, 133
    vanilla poached, 119
pineapple, chocolate-dipped
    with honey-raspberry sauce,
        127
sauces for, 134–36
strawberry omelet with
    nectarine sauce, 122–23
Dessert sauces, 122, 124, 126,
    134–36
    apricot-orange, 126
    carob hot fudge, 135
    honey-raspberry, 136
    maple hot chocolate, 134–36
    nectarine, 122
    orange-raisin, 124
Dip(s):
    curried yogurt, 38
    peanut chili, 37
Do-ahead party buffet menu, 142
Dressings for salads. See Salad
    dressings

Eggplant and seasame cream, 31
Eggs, 3
Egg sauce, 114
Entertaining, 138
Entrees, 81–116
    asparagus-cashew stir-fry,
        100–01
    chef's garden skillet, 112–13
    chick pea-zucchini curry, 87
    couscous with egg sauce and
        garden vegetables, 114–15
    frittata, 108–09
    macaroni
        and cheese with vegetables,
            92
        Parmesan herbed, 93

nut burgers, 116
omelet(s)
    curry-chutney, 104
    fillings and sauce
        combinations, 102–07
    frittata, 108–09
    guacamole, 106–07
    ideas for, 105
    noodle, 102–03
    tomato-pesto, 105
    tomato-ricotta, 103
pasta
    with Chinese tahini sauce, 88
    with herbed ricotta and pine
        nuts, 85
    marinara on beds of spinach,
        90
    al pesto, 84
    with ricotta-walnut sauce, 86
    shells with lemon vinaigrette,
        82–83
    with Szechwan peanut
        dressing, 89
rice
    stir-fried, 110
    and vegetable skillet, 111
sweet and sour tofu, 94–95
tacos, 113–14
triple cheese–poppyseed
    noodles, 91
vegetable
    curry, 96–97
    stir-fry with ginger sauce, 98–
        99
Equipment for cooking, 6–7

Fall luncheon menu, 141
Family dinner menu, 142
Fats, 3, 5
    moderation and, 5
    monosaturated, 3
    saturated, 3
    unsaturated, 3
Festive omelet dinner menu, 142
Fifteen-minute cooking, 5–10, 11–
    28

basic foods for, 11–28
basics, on-hand supply of, 6
broiling, 8
chopping by hand, 8
cold-tossing, 8
equipment for, 6–7
food processing and, 7–8
microwaving, 8–9
oils, 10
organized kitchens and, 6
presentation planning and, 6
pressure cooking, 9
sautéeing, 8
scrambling, 8
steaming, 8
stir-frying, 8
stocking the pantry, 9–10
ten techniques for, 7–9
ten tips for, 7
weekly plan, 6
See also Vegetarian cooking
Fluffy strawberry omelet with
nectarine sauce, 122–23
Food combinations (proteins), 3
grains and legumes, 3
grains and milk products, 3
seeds and legumes, 3
Food processing, 7–8
blenders and, 7
selecting a processor, 7–8
Four basic food groups, 4
variety and, 4
French potato salad with savory
vinaigrette, 66
Fresh ingredients *vs.* frozen or
canned, 9
Frittata, 108–09
Frozen banana-berry parfaits,
131
Fruit, 118, 125, 132
curried, 125
as dessert, 118
smoothie, 132
Fruit salad
with curried yogurt dressing,
62

and sprouts with gingered
yogurt dressing, 63

Garlic-tomato sauce, 25
Garnishes, 6
Gazpacho, 48
Gingered yogurt dressing,
63
Ginger sauce, 28
Glazed oranges, 128
Grains, 14–15
bulgur wheat, 15
couscous, 15
and legumes, 3
and milk products, 3
millet, 15
rice, 14
Guacamole omelet with tomato
hot sauce, 106–07

Herbed garlic croutons, 51
Herbed macaroni Parmesan, 93
Herbed tomato sauce, 75
Honey
-mustard dressing, 58
-poppyseed dressing, 57
-raspberry sauce, 136
Hot pepper vinaigrette, 77
Hummus, 32

Indonesian vegetable salad, 64
Italian dressing, creamy, 76
Italian garden frittata, 108–09

Knives, 6, 8
chopping with, 8
technique for using, 8

Label reading, 9
Leftovers, 10
Legumes, 17
combining for protein, 17
preparing and cooking, 17
yield of dry beans, 17
Lemon salad dressing, 72
Lemon vinaigrette, 83

Light and fresh feast, 141
Light pesto vinaigrette, 23, 68

Macaroni
and cheese with vegetables, 92
Parmesan, herbed, 93
Maple
hot chocolate sauce, 134
oranges amandine, 130
Marinara sauce, 24
Mayonnaise, 20
Meatless mission chili, 42
Menu Italiano, 142
Menu samples, 141–42
Microwaving, 8–9
Milk, 3
Millet, 15
Mixed fruit chutney, 21
Moderation, 4–5
additives and, 5
excesses and, 4
fats and, 5
salt and, 4–5
sugar and, 5
Monosaturated fats, 3
Morning glory brunch menu, 142
Moroccan chick pea soup, 47
Mustard, 19

Nectarine sauce, 122
Noodle(s)
omelet, 102–03
Thai salad, 78
triple cheese–poppyseed, 91
Nut burgers, 116

Oils, 3, 10
cold-pressed, 10
olive oil, 10
sesame oil, 10
Olive oil, 10
Omelet(s), 18, 102–07
adding fillings to, 18
for a crowd, 18
curry-chutney, 104

Omelet(s) (continued)
 fluffy, 18
 French, 18
 frittata, 108–09
 guacamole, 106–07
 ideas for, 105
 noodle, 102–03
 ricotta filling in, 103
 tomato-pesto, 105
 tomato-ricotta, 103
Orange(s)
 glazed, 128
 maple, amandine, 130
 -tahini sauce, 27
 -raisin sauce, 124
Organized kitchens, 6
Oriental potato salad with soy
   dressing, 67
Oriental rice and vegetable
   skillet, 111
Oriental stew, 40–41
Oriental stir-fried rice, 110
Oriental vinaigrette, 70
Osteoporosis, 4

Pasta
 -asparagus salad, 74–75
 and bean soup, 46
 with Chinese tahini sauce, 88
 and couscous salad with spicy
   peanut dressing, 79–80
 with herbed ricotta and pine
   nuts, 85
 marinara on beds of spinach,
   90
 al pesto, 84
 picnic menu, 142
 with ricotta-walnut sauce, 86
 salad primavera, 73, 74
 shells with lemon vinaigrette,
   82–83
 with Szechwan peanut
   dressing, 89
 Szechwan salad, with hot
   pepper vinaigrette, 77
 See also Pasta (generally)

Pasta (generally), 15–16
 calories in, 15
 cooking ahead, 16
 described, 15
 how to cook, 15–16
 servings for, 4, 16
 "sizers," 15
 See also Pasta
Peach(es)
 baked, with chutney stuffing,
   121
 Melba, 123
 vinaigrette, 60
Peanut
 chili dip, 36
 dressing, spicy, 79
 sauce, 28
 Szechwan, 89
Pear(s)
 poached Alaska, 120
 ricotta-topped, 129
 sorbet, 133
 vanilla poached, 119
Pea soup, quick, 43
Pepper vinaigrette, 61
Pesto, 22–23
 basic, 22
 herb spread, 23
 light vinaigrette, 23, 68
 spinach-parsley, 23
 uses for, 23
Pineapple chocolate-dipped,
   with honey-raspberry sauce,
   127
Pita crisps, 52
Planning meals, 139–42
 menu planning, 141
 sample menus, 141–42
 tips on complete meals, 140
Poached pears Alaska, 120
Potato salad
 with light pesto vinaigrette,
   68
 with savory vinaigrette, 66
 with soy dressing, 67
Presentation, planning of, 6

Pressure cooking, 9
Protein, 2–3, 4
 American diet and, 2
 in dairy products, 4
 eggs, milk, and tofu, 3
 food combinations, 3
 grains and milk products, 3
 in vegetarian diet, 3
Pureed vegetable soup with
   broccoli florets, 44–45

Quick pea soup, 43

Raw and cooked foods, balance
   between, 4
Rice
 and spinach salad, with oriental
   vinaigrette, 70–71
 and vegetable skillet, 111
 See also Rice (generally)
Rice (generally), 14–15
 Basmati, 14
 how to cook, 14–15
 long-grain brown, 14
 reheating, 14
 storing, 14
 variations, 14–15
 white, 14
 See also Rice
Ricotta
 -topped pears, 129
 -walnut sauce, 86

Salad(s), 51–53, 55–80
 accompaniments for, 51–53
 almond butter–wheat germ
   sticks for, 52-53
 basil bean, 69
 couscous-currant, with lemon
   dressing, 72–73
 croutons for, 51
 cucumber, 65
 fruit and sprout, with gingered
   yogurt dressing, 63
 Indonesian vegetable, 64

pasta
-asparagus, 74–75
and couscous, with spicy
peanut dressing, 79–80
primavera, 73–74
Szechwan, with hot pepper
vinaigrette, 77
pita crisps for, 52
potato salad
with light pesto vinaigrette,
68
with savory vinaigrette, 66
with soy dressing, 67
rice and spinach, with oriental
vinaigrette, 70–71
spinach and strawberry, with
pepper vinaigrette, 61
teriyaki, 71
Thai noodle, 78
tossed green, 56–60
winter fruit salad with curried
yogurt dressing, 62
See also Salad dressing(s);
Tossed green salads
Salad dressing(s), 57–60
apple, 59
chutney, 60
creamy Italian, 76
curried yogurt dressing, 62
gingered yogurt dressing, 63
herbed tomato sauce, 75
honey-mustard, 58
honey-poppyseed, 57
hot pepper vinaigrette, 77
lemon, 72
light pesto vinaigrette, 68
oriental vinaigrette, 70
peach vinaigrette, 60
pepper vinaigrette, 61
savory vinaigrette, 66
sesame soy, 58
soy dressing, 67
spicy peanut, 79
Szechwan peanut, 79
vinaigrette, 59
yogurt-Parmesan, 76

Salt, 2, 4–5
daily requirement for, 4
excessive intake of, 4
Sample menus, 141–42
Saturated fats, 3
Sauce(s), 24–28
egg, 114
garlic-tomato, 25
ginger, 28
marinara, 24
orange-tahini, 27
peanut, 28
ricotta-walnut, 86
sweet and sour, 94
tahini, Chinese, 88
tomato
herbed, 75
-yogurt, 26
zesty, 26
See also Dessert sauces
Sautéed apple slices with apricot-
orange sauce, 126
Sautéeing, 8
Savory nut burgers, 116
Savory vinaigrette dressing,
66
Scrambling, 8
Seeds and legumes, 3
Sesame oil, 10
Sesame soy dressing, 58
Simple carbohydrates, 3
Simple soup dinner menu,
141
Soup(s), 39–53
accompaniments for, 51–53
almond butter–wheat germ
sticks for, 52–53
blueberry, 50
carrot, 45
chick pea, 47
croutons for, 51
gazpacho, 48
meatless mission chili, 42
oriental stew, 40–41
pasta and bean, 46
pita crisps for, 5

strawberry, 49
vegetable, puréed with broccoli
florets, 44–45
Southeast Asian dinner menu,
141
Soy dressing, 67
Spicy peanut dressing, 79
Spinach
-parsley pesto, 23
and strawberry salad with
pepper vinaigrette, 61
Staples in stock, 9
Steaming, 8
Stir-frying, 8
Stir-fry spiced menu, 142
Stock. See Vegetable stock
Stocking the pantry, 9–10
dried herbs, 9
fresh, frozen, or canned
vegetables, 9
labels, reading of, 9
leftovers, 10
staples, 9
vegetable stock and, 9
Strawberry
omelet with nectarine sauce,
122–23
soup, 49
Sugar, 5
excess consumption of, 5
Summer peach vinaigrette, 60
Sweet and sour sauce, 94
Sweet and sour tofu, 94–95
Szechwan pasta salad with hot
pepper vinaigrette, 77
Szechwan peanut dressing, 89

Tacos, 113–14
Tahini
Chinese sauce, 88
-orange sauce, 27
Tangy honey-mustard dressing,
58
Ten techniques of food
preparation, 7–9
broiling, 8

Ten techniques of food
    preparation (*continued*)
  chopping by hand, 8
  cold-tossing, 8
  food processing, 7–8
  microwaving, 8–9
  pressure cooking, 9
  sautéeing, 8
  scrambling, 8
  steaming, 8
  stir-frying, 8
Ten tips for 15-minute cooking,
    7
Thai cucumber salad, 65
Thai noodle salad, 78
Tofu, 3, 34–35
  batter-dipped, 34–35
Tomato
  -pesto omelet, 105
  -ricotta omelet, 103
  sauce
    herbed, 75
    yogurt, 26
    zesty, 26
Tossed green salads, 56–60
  dressings for, 57–60
  greens for, 57
  low-calorie additives, 57
  miscellaneous additions to, 57
  preparing, 56–57
  protein additives, 57
Triple cheese–poppyseed
    noodles, 91

Unsaturated fats, 3

Vanilla poached pears, 119
Variety in meals, 4
  fiber and, 4
  four basic food groups and,
    4
Vegetable(s):
  chef's garden skillet, 112–13
  curry, 96–97
  soup, pureed with broccoli
    florets, 44–45
  spread, cheesy, 33
  stir-fry with ginger sauce, 98–
    99
Vegetable stock, 9, 12–13
  herbs for, 9
  powder, 9, 12
  recipe for, 13
Vegetarian cooking, 1–28
  accompaniments for soups and
    salads, 51–53
  appetizers, 29–37
  balance and, 2–4
  basic foods of, 11–28
  carbohydrates and, 3
  dairy products and, 4
  desserts, 117–36
  entertaining and, 138
  entrees, 81–116
  fats and, 3
  fiber and, 4
  fifteen-minute cooking, 5–10
  four basic food groups and, 4
  "gourmet approach" to, 2
  mail order sources for, 114
  moderation and, 4–5

  planning and, 139–42
  principles of, 2–5
  protein and, 2–3, 4
  raw and cooked foods, 4
  reasons for, 2
  salad dressings, 57–80
  salads, 55–80
  salt and, 2
  soups, 39–53
  "total vegetarianism," 2
  variety and, 4
  water and, 3–4
  See also Fifteen-minute cooking
Vegetarian tacos, 113–14
Vinaigrette dressing(s):
  basic, 59
  hot pepper, 77
  lemon, 83
  light pesto, 68
  oriental, 70
  peach, 60
  pepper, 61
  savory, 66

Water, 3–4
  in fruits and vegetables, 3–4
Weekly plan, 6
  advance planning and, 6
Winter carrot soup, 45
Winter fruit salad with curried
    yogurt dressing, 62

Yogurt
  dip, curried, 37
  -Parmesan dressing, 76